MP 11 $9 95

FLOWER DECORATION

FLOWER DECORATION

By
CONSTANCE SPRY

With a Preface by
MICHELE TUCKER

and a Foreword by
SIR WILLIAM LAWRENCE

745.92
Spry, Constance, 1886-1960.
Flower decoration

Academy Chicago Publishers

Published by
Academy Chicago Publishers
213 West Institute Place
Chicago, IL 60610

Copyright © 1993 by Academy Chicago Publishers

No part of this book may be reproduced in any form without the express written permission of the publisher.

Printed and bound in the USA

CONTENTS

CHAP.		PAGE
	Preface . . . . Michele Tucker	1
	Foreword . . . . William Lawrence	xv
I.	Introduction	1
II.	Table Decorations	8
III.	The Mixed Bunch	24
IV.	White Flowers	30
V.	Green and Grey	44
VI.	Red and Pink	52
VII.	Yellow, Gold, Cream, and Brown	62
VIII.	Blue Flowers	72
IX.	Flowers for Weddings	80
X.	Decorations for Christmas, for Parties, and for Restaurants	89
XI.	Vases	96
XII.	Aids to Flower Arrangements and Methods of Preserving them—London Gardens	102
	Appendix	109
	Illustrations (*from photographs by Paul Lait*)	121

ACKNOWLEDGEMENTS

It would not have been possible to write the preface to a book of this nature, nor indeed to have reprinted the book itself, without the help of many experts at horticultural centers across the country. First, a special thanks to Roy L. Taylor, Ph. D., Director of the Chicago Botanic Garden, who allowed me access to the Garden library's unique specialized collection. Also, I am grateful to Dr Michael Stieber of the Morton Arboretum, who arranged permission to print from their copy of *Flower Decoration*. He and his staff at the Sterling Library, especially Mr Peter Wang, were most helpful and gracious, and their collection of early gardening journals was indispensable. I must also thank Allan Kramer of the Brooklyn Botanic Garden for kindly gathering the particulars of Mrs Spry's engagement there; Susan Fraser at the New York Botanic Garden for unearthing Mrs Spry's newsletter in the special archives; and Michelle Carver at the Center for Research Libraries for her assistance. Many thanks are due my friends, without whom I could not have reached these far-flung libraries. And to Anita Miller, for being so receptive to the idea of this book, for giving me the opportunity to write the preface, and for her valuable guidance, I am most grateful.

Michele Tucker
Chicago, Illinois
November 1992

PREFACE

In January 1938, the Women's Auxiliary of the Brooklyn Botanic Garden achieved a considerable coup when Mrs Constance Spry, in her first American appearances, gave two talks at their annual benefit. Mrs Spry was the darling of the British aristocracy; her clients included the Duchesses of Kent, Gloucester, Norfolk and Roxburgh, as well as the Duke of Windsor, both when he was Prince of Wales and when he was King. Her services were in demand for society events and weddings, the most recent of which was the Duke's marriage to Mrs Simpson. And renowned for her revolutionary floral arrangements in the very visible windows of chic Atkinsons scent shop on Bond Street, she could claim, without doubt, the title of "the first superstar florist."* Constance Spry was an archetype.

In America, however, the archetype was about to encounter some unimagined resistance to her floral philosophy. Although her arrangements were eclectic and unorthodox, they were firmly rooted in the European, or Western tradition. But it was the Japanese, or Eastern tradition which prevailed among members of the Garden Clubs of America, who sponsored Mrs Spry's tour. Julia Berrall points out that "when the garden-club movement really got going into full swing . . . in the 1920s, members began looking for rules [of flower arrangement, accepting many] verbatim from the Japanese."

That Mrs Spry may have startled some of her audience at the Botanic Garden Benefit is evident from press comments on the event, as well as her own remarks after the tour. *The New York Herald Tribune* headlined its January 26th article: "Kale Bouqets Found to Tickle British Fancy . . . Decorator for Windsors Uses Vegetables or Weeds if They're Ornamental . . . She Glorifies the Tomato, Rhubarb and Artichoke." No one, evidently, threw any tomatoes at her, but after her lecture someone pointedly asked ". . .whether she ever had garnished

i

*Jody Shields, p. 28

the walls of Fort Belvedere with kale." She responded that she couldn't recall offhand, but that "kale and rhododendron made a nice combination...." She recalled afterwards in *Garden Notebook,* "When I first came to America I was laughed at quite a lot for introducing vegetable leaves and fruits into my flower arrangements. Provided the plant is beautiful, I cannot see why I should not use it for decoration just because it has the added advantage that it can also be eaten."

Her style did not shock everyone in the country; she was introduced at the Botanic Garden luncheon by Richardson Wright, editor of *House and Garden* and secretary of the New York Horticultural Society. *House and Garden,* in fact, ran an article later that year boasting of an American woman who used kale on her table "...long before Mrs Constance Spry landed on our shores to tell us the success story of the humble *Brassica oleracea* in London, England." And this same article refers with disdain to "...the Garden Club trumpeters with their tape measures and solemn judges," who so zealously implemented the Eastern standards.

Constance Spry had dismissed Japanese floral arrangement in her introduction to this very book, *Flower Decoration,* first published in 1934. "Beautiful as many Japanese arrangements are, and greatly as they must suit the background they find in their own country, I doubt if they are really suitable for us in England."

After her American tour, in her 1940 *Garden Notebook* , she re-addressed the issue with a hint of impatience:

> I genuinely admire the exquisite examples of flower arrangement that I see in America, but while I admire this very highly specialized art and like delicate arrangements, and precise arrangements, . . .every now and then I lose patience and want to sweep everything finicking aside...Am I wrong or is there a frequent and insistent Oriental influence shown in the flower arrangements of women who would not think of furnishing their rooms in Japanese furniture or dressing exclusively in kimonos? ...aren't things just a bit stereotyped here and there? I want to shout out: 'Do what you please, follow your own star, be Oriental if you want to be and don't if you don't want to be...'

PREFACE

She would continue to rail against rules for the rest of her life, and her biographer remarks that while "Constance was always careful to pay lip-service to the charm of Oriental styles, . . .temperamentally she was not attuned to its austerities; her instinct was always for the billowing and the lavish."

Under these circumstances, it is amusing to note that during Mrs Spry's address to the Women's Auxiliary, the Japanese shrine at the Brooklyn Botanic Garden was burned to the ground. "There is no room for doubt that this was an anti-Japanese demonstration. . ." said the director of the Botanic Garden, in attendance at the Waldorf-Astoria luncheon at the time of the fire. Luckily, Mrs Spry had a good alibi.

It is easy to understand her frustration, because the two main trends in flower decoration, stemming from the East and from the West, could almost be said to be diametrically opposed. The visual difference alone between the stark, formal, stylized arrangements of the East, and the profuse, colorful, jam-packed and overflowing arrangements of the West, typified by Dutch still-lifes, is obvious to even the most casual observer. But what is less obviously understood is that the two trends developed as they did for very different reasons. While Western floral art is essentially decorative, Eastern floral art is above all symbolic; its decorative qualities are incidental to its symbolic intent.

Influenced by Buddhism and the teachings of Confucius, Japanese floral art went through various incarnations, from what Julia Berrall calls "a highly stylized and formal temple art" with arrangements reaching forty feet and often taking days to complete, to the smaller arrangements Mrs Spry encountered, concerned with three main lines that observed strict placement requirements and proportional relationships.

The garden-clubs' wholesale adoption of so foreign and stylized an art may just have been a younger culture's efforts to emulate an older culture's achievements, or it may have been part of the American craze for all things Japanese. Whatever the reasons, a flurry of books appeared in the thirties singing the praises of Japanese floral arrangement. Mrs. Walter Hine wrote, "It is only within the last ten years or so that the occidental public has been sufficiently interested in flower arrangement as an art, to want or ask for some rules or standards of excellence. . . .only in Japan has the art been fostered and developed to its highest degree of perfection."

And J. Gregory Conway commented:

> In her careful consideration of the moods of nature Japan knows little of the cloak of superficiality which, since the Renaissance, has overlain Western civilization. The Eastern placement of flowers had been as devotedly studied as the Western has been negligently casual. Where the Oriental has selected his material with unerring accuracy for its fitness in his design, the Occidental all too often has made haphazard choice from the blossoms nearest at hand

Perhaps there was a feeling that America was aesthetically inferior to Japan; maybe a puritanical streak caused a reaction against any easy enjoyment of flowers. Differences between East and West were framed as moral issues. This American approach to flower arrangement as an intimidating or exclusive refinement was quite unlike Mrs Spry's attitude, "I want nobody to be left out where flowers are concerned."

In 1952 her inclusive tendencies were again in evidence when, in remarks to the Royal Horticultural Society, Mrs Spry praised what she felt was the one positive aspect of the American Garden Society movement. She recalled her pleasure at her extraordinary discovery on her American tour that "...people who did not garden at all and who had not got gardens [took] such a big part in the Garden Societies in America..." She felt that this was an aspect of the phenomenon the burgeoning English flower arrangement societies could adopt, because "...there are a great many people, particularly women, who for one reason or another cannot garden, and I do not see why they should not be encouraged to join in the extreme pleasure to be derived from these flower activities." She welcomed the development of flower arranging societies not only because they provided an infusion of "new blood" but because they promised to "fill a real need, particularly for women" as a "means of self-expression." However, she expressed reservations about certain aspects of American Garden Societies which, her biographer says, were "primarily social, not horticultural...the possession of a large drawing room where fund-raising meetings could be held [being] a better qualification than green fingers." With a cautionary tale about an American newlywed who was afraid to arrange

PREFACE

flowers for her appreciative husband if any Garden Society member might be likely to see them, Mrs Spry commented:

> It would never do for us to get into that state of mind. . . .It will not be at all a good idea if a society springs up and lays down such stiff rules that people are frightened off. . . .There is a danger here, as will be realized by anybody who has seen American shows; there is a tendency in the United States to have one sort of decoration suitable for show and another kind for the home—which does not seem to me to be satisfactory . . .if one starts such a society, the doors must be kept wide open, and everybody encouraged to come in. Above all, we have to be careful that we do not make too many rules and get ourselves tangled up by the rule makers. It is a curious thing that sometimes when a new society is started, somebody springs up and says, 'Now let us make the rules.'

Mrs Spry disliked the American clubs' undemocratic treatment not only of people, but of flower-arrangements as well. Their show conventions excluded the background of the average American interior as context for arrangements, and they stipulated that certain plant and flowering materials could not be mixed within the arrangements themselves. Mrs Spry believed in any means of achieving her desired aesthetic effect.

The restrictive rules of the American garden club movement virtually eliminated the entire tradition in which she worked, and precluded her famous innovations with which she redefined the Western tradition of floral arrangement. Confining her to the American approach would have been the equivalent of telling the Impressionists they could paint only in black and white.

Constance Spry came of age just after the turn of the century in England, an auspicious time for a new approach. Hers is an art rooted deeply in the Western tradition, nourished by the Arts and Crafts movement, and very much a part of the natural approach to gardening; a trend which could be said to be the precursor of today's politically correct wildflower garden.

The Western tradition began in the Middle Ages, when the earliest gardens were tended by monks behind the safety of monastery walls. Stocked with herbs, fruits, and vegetables, for use either as food or medicine, these utilitarian gardens did include some flowers purely for beauty or scent. But not until the fifteenth and sixteenth centuries did real flower gardening begin, says Julia Berrall, when "...the fortress town [gave way] to individual homes," and life became sufficiently secure for the planting of individual lawns, kitchen gardens, and purely decorative gardens.

In the seventeenth and eighteenth centuries, horticultural knowledge greatly increased because of overseas trading and colonization by the seafaring powers of Holland and England. The result of so much plant exploration, classification, and propagation, says Berrall, was that by the nineteenth century, "... gardening was practiced to some extent by everyone who owned a plot of ground." And Victorian gardening did not even require plots of ground, because greenhouse construction increased after the glass tax was lifted in 1845.

In 1886, when Constance Spry was born, the fashion in gardens was the "bedding out" or "carpet-bedding" system, named after the practice of raising brightly colored tropical flowers in greenhouses so that they could be set out in elaborate geometric flower beds for a brief time in summer, only to have to be dug up in fall. The flowers were kept at a uniform height, hence the "carpet" analogy.

Inside the Victorian home, the fern craze was in full bloom. Thirty-seven species of fern had been introduced to England in 1795 by William Bligh, captain of the *Bounty*. Factory smoke and fumes had made their survival in city soil difficult until, quite by accident, Nathaniel Ward developed his glass fern case when a fern sprouted in a bottle he was using to incubate a moth.

Gardeners Magazine, the arbiter of *nouveau* middle-class Victorian taste, praised the Wardian cases for their ability to preserve plants in rooms and in cities, and recommended the use of these miniature conservatories as "substitutes for bad views or for no views at all." This use of plants as camouflage for surroundings was a practice Constance Spry would sweep away.

Not only plants camouflaged the Victorian interior; so did the mass-produced bric-a-brac popularized in part by the Great Exhibition of 1851, which heralded the new technological age. While ferns and other plants were believed to purify the air, bric-a-brac had no such redemptive value.

"The two great crusaders against the shoddy materialism of the Victorian

PREFACE

Age were John Ruskin and William Morris",* both of whom greatly influenced Constance Spry's revolutionary predecessors: Gertrude Jekyll and William Robinson. Ruskin (1819-1908) lamented the coldness and lack of humanity in objects churned out from factories in undeviating patterns, believing that quality was a manifestation of the personal touch and imagination of the craftsperson. His aesthetic philosophy depended upon a return to nature; he rejected the machine.

William Morris (1834-96) put Ruskin's tenets into practice and inspired the Arts and Crafts movement, which took its name from the Arts and Crafts Exhibition of 1888. This movement emphasized the superior quality of indigenous handmade crafts, promoting the "unity of all the aesthetic arts." And it was Gertrude Jekyll (1843-1932) who "brought gardening into this movement."* She had been an accomplished painter and craftswoman before deteriorating eyesight caused her to incorporate her interests into garden design, where she was to make her most significant contribution. In 1875 she met William Robinson, who was already well-known because of his book *The Wild Garden* (1870). They had much in common, and she became a frequent contributor to his magazine *The Garden*. Both abhorred Victorian carpet-bedding, with its garish color combinations and preoccupation with novelty; Robinson was outraged that "all true plant form was banished because it did not fit into the carpet pattern!" Jekyll and Robinson believed that "planting should be suited to the land and to the natural growth, and plants should look as though they had a right to be there."* This return to naturalism was part of the Arts and Crafts idealization of country life and old-fashioned cottage gardens, which bloomed year round, and in order to achieve this natural, continuous bloom, Robinson advocated the use of herbaceous perennials and bulbs.

But it was Robinson's polemical work *The English Flower Garden* (1883), which evolved from articles in *The Garden*, that became one of the earth-shaking forces in the history of gardening, rousing the majority of gardeners who, up until then, were in thrall to the conventions of carpet-bedding. And it was Gertrude Jekyll who wrote its chapter on colour. Jekyll was influenced as an art student by a work which was to influence the entire Arts and Crafts movement, as well as the Impressionist painters: Michel Chevreul's *The Principles of Harmony and Contrast of Colours, and their Application to the Arts*, translated into English in

*Mavis Batey, p. 17-21

1854. Michel Chevreul (1786-1889) had been Director of Tints at the Gobelin Tapestry factory in Paris and

> observed in his work what the eye actually perceived in colour. Here are to be found many of Miss Jekyll's planting ideas—no one colour is seen alone, colour is affected by colours around it, white flowers are the only ones that possess the advantage of heightening the tone of flowers which have only a light tint of colour, grey helps all colours gain in purity and brilliance.*

Jekyll translated the Impressionists' painting technique into flower borders, "where the petals or the flowers themselves were the equivalent of ...brushstrokes."†

Not only did Gertrude Jekyll work with colour interdependency, but she created, with the architect Sir Edwin Lutyens,‡ a unity of house and garden. They gave "the new century a new style which would reconcile architects, gardeners, craftsmen and the rival merits of formal design and natural planting."* And into this unified, naturalized garden, grown free from the arbitrary and unnatural conventions which constrained it prior to Robinson/ Jekyll/ Lutyens, stepped Constance Spry.

She is their ideological heir in many ways, and in her own way she revolutionized the art of flower decoration. Ignoring do's and don'ts, she swept aside fusty Victorian decorations still in vogue in the 1920s, clearing tables swathed in bowers of greenery and garlands of smilax, and interiors camouflaged by ferns.

Just as Robinson had advocated consideration of topography in planning a garden, Mrs Spry advocated consideration of the room itself in the placement of floral décor. She felt, says her biographer, that "...no decorative art can be satisfactorily practiced separate from its setting," and that "the intrinsic beauty of the building should be enhanced, not obscured; or, if it were an ugly one...the flowers should distract attention from its ugly features, not attempt to cover them up."

Hers was an interdependent approach between setting and décor in keeping with that of Jekyll and Lutyens towards house and garden. She broke down

---

*Mavis Batey, pp. 17-21
†Judith Tankard, p. 16
‡It is interesting to note that Mrs Spry's access, as a floral decorator, to the fashionable churches in London was occasioned by the wedding of Sir Edwin Lutyens' daughter, Mary, at the insistence of his wife, Lady Emily.

barriers between the kitchen garden and the cutting garden; as Beverley Nichols put it, she was "the first floral artist who ever walked straight from the herbaceous border to the cabbage patch." Seasons were no obstacle to her, either: ". . .she has opened the doors which kept us inside during the winter months, and shown us the delights that await us in the bleakest hedgerows on the darkest days. . .pale, spectral leaves, withered seedpods, berries of black and purple, bare branches."

Her debt to Jekyll is evident in her own sensitivity to interdependent colour effect, within arrangements and within rooms. She notes in *Party Flowers*, for example, that "green, a lovely colour in itself, has the effect of cooling down other colours," and the brilliance of "a pool of golden marigolds" in a "dull or cold room," will be heightened "by the degree to which you dispense with their green leaves. . .and strengthen the effect of colour and warmth by the addition of coloured leaves." This use of foliage was far more sophisticated than the role it played before she came on the scene, when leaves were used "as material of secondary importance. . .for filling up the back of a vase or to hide gaps in a faulty arrangement."

Mrs Spry overturned the prejudice against all-white arrangements, which had been primarily reserved for funerals, and made them fashionable in the famous all-white rooms of interior decorator Syrie Maugham. "Rightly used and placed, white flowers are not cold, but a high light; not colourless but infinitely delicately shot through with tinted light and in some cases faintly reflective of the colour surrounding them," said Mrs Spry. Hers is an Impressionist understanding of white, and she also had an Impressionist appreciation of the effect of light on a composition's colour, due to the unique translucence of petals.

If all this sounds very painterly, it is because Constance Spry aspired to use flowers, she said, "as an artist would use colors," viewing the whole room as a canvas, and the flowers as part of the overall scheme of decoration. She wanted to achieve the same "thrill of the beholder" achieved by the great Dutch and Flemish painters with their still-lifes. Her biographer notes her "girlhood familiarity" with the work of these artists, from the time her father thought her artistic tendencies might express themselves in paint. Happily for the floral world, she couldn't draw.

Born in Derby in 1886, she grew up in Ireland, where her father was Chief Inspector of Technical Education. After one year at college she became the first full-time paid lecturer of the Women's National Health Association, whose goal was to "alleviate Irish poverty and distress."* In 1910 she married James Hepple Marr, a mining engineer, with whom she had a son, Anthony. She left her husband in 1916 and returned to England where, as Director of Women's Staff at the Aircraft Production Department, she met her second husband, Shav Spry, the department's Head of Personnel. After the war, when she became headmistress at Homerton School, news of her way with flowers spread, and people began asking her to do arrangements for their dinner parties. At one of these parties she met Norman Wilkinson, a theatrical designer, whose painting she had admired in *The Studio* magazine when she was a girl.

He was designing a scent shop, Atkinsons, that "would be quite unlike any shop that had ever been,"* and for which he wanted flowers quite unlike any florist's flowers that had ever been. He immediately insisted she do the flowers for Atkinsons and encouraged her to turn professional, which she was able to do in 1928. She opened her own shop, called Floral Decorations to distinguish it from ordinary floristry, and Atkinsons became her main client. There she had her "window on the world", where she pioneered her work with unusual containers, assisted by Wilkinson's theatrical eye and his junk-shop treasures. Mrs Spry's biographer remembers:

> No one going up or down Bond Street could possibly miss Atkinsons, and the flower arrangements were spotlit at night. [They] stood as if on the stage of a theatre…And people did notice, did stop and stare. Those great groups, majestic yet ethereal, were totally unlike anything that had been seen before, different in colouring, in blending of materials, above all in line."

Her success allowed her to increase her staff and move her shop to a better address—two doors up from Atkinsons. In 1934, the year in which she wrote *Flower Decoration*, she did flowers for her first royal client, the Duke of Kent. And around this time she opened the Constance Spry Flower School, for

---

*Elizabeth Coxhead, p. 52

PREFACE

debutantes as well as professional aspirants who could help staff her shop.

In 1935 she did her first royal wedding, and the Prince of Wales became a regular client. Her 1938 American tour culminated in an offer of a shop in New York, backed by some society hostesses who, according to her biographer, wanted Mrs Spry to "revolutionize the American House and Garden." The war prevented her from returning to New York as planned, and so the shop, Constance Spry Inc., was eventually sold. In 1945 she opened Winkfield, a school which offered courses in such skills as cooking, housekeeping, flower decoration and gardening; its principle aim was to teach its students to run civilized homes. She was involved also in the Chelsea Flower Show, and in the events which led to the formation of the National Association of Flower Arrangement Societies of Great Britain. She wrote thirteen books and a prodigious number of articles. She had the honour of doing the flowers for Princess Elizabeth's wedding in Westminster Abbey, but she felt her greatest triumph came in 1953 with the assignment to do the flowers along the processional route of the Coronation. Her desire to reach everyone with flowers could not have been given a better arena and, as a result of this service, she received the Order of the British Empire.

In 1959 she gave an Australian lecture tour. Still true to her principles, she said, "Beware of stylizing. Accept no rules. Let the flowers remind you of how they looked when growing. You are not human unless you have a way of expressing yourself." She died at Winkfield on January 3, 1960.

In the preface to this, her first book, Sir William Lawrence writes, "I feel I am in the position of the Archbishop of Canterbury if he were asked to write a Foreward to the Bible; every word is gospel to me." He credits Constance Spry with "precipitating an aesthetic renaissance."

America today, poised at the turn of a new century, is experiencing a new appreciation of nature and the environment not at all unlike the reaction to the Industrial Revolution which precipitated the Arts and Crafts movement and the Spry phenomenon. We too are experiencing a *fin de siècle* flurry of design activity, in artist created decorative painting techniques for the home, and in the surge of interest in the garden.

Let us hope we are now ready to appreciate and join in the flowering renaissance which Mrs Spry tried to introduce here half a century ago. And may her opening remarks in this book serve as a warning against rules and pronouncements, as encouragement to all, and as a reminder that the very best amongst us are often the least pretentious: ". . .because of the infinite variety of material and the limitless scope for the expression of individual tastes, the last word is never said."

WORKS CONSULTED

Allen, David Elliston. *The Victorian Fern Craze: A History of Pteridomania.* London: Hutchinson and Company, Ltd, 1969.

Batey, Mavis. "Gertrude Jekyll and the Arts and Crafts Movement", in *Gertrude Jekyll: Artist, Gardener, Craftswoman.* ed. M.J. Tooley. Witton-le-Wear, U.K.: Michaelmas Books, 1984.

Berrall, Julia. *A History of Flower Arrangement.* NY: Alfred A. Knopf, 1940.

Brown, Jane. *Gardens of a Golden Afternoon: The Story of a Partnership: Edwin Lutyens and Gertrude Jekyll.* NY: Van Nostrand Reinhold Co, 1982.

Conway, J. Gregory. *Flowers: East-West.* NY: Alfred A. Knopf, 1939.

Coxhead, Elizabeth. *Constance Spry: A Biography.* London: Wm. Luscombe Publisher Ltd, 1975.

Hine, Mrs Walter R. *The Arrangement of Flowers.* NY: Charles Scribner's Sons, 1933.

Nichols, Beverly, foreword to *The Art of Arranging Flowers* by Constance Spry. NY: The Studio Publications, Inc. / Thomas Y. Crowell Co, n.d.

Robinson, William. *The English Flower Garden.* NY: The Amaryllis Press, 1984.

Shields, Jody. "Revolution in Bloom", *HG* (Feb. 1992), pp. 28-30, 32.

Spry, Constance. *Constance Spry's Garden Notebook.* NY: Alfred A. Knopf, 1940.

___. "Flower Arrangement", *Journal of the Royal Horticultural Society,* LXXVII (1952), pp. 268-70.

___. *Party Flowers.* NY: The Studio Publications Inc. / Thomas Y. Crowell Co., n.d.

Tankard, Judith B. and Michael R. Van Valkenburgh. *Gertrude Jekyll: A Vision of Garden and Wood.* NY: Harry N. Abrams, Inc./Sagapress, Inc., 1989.

Thomas, Ethel Dodd. "Revolution in Flower Arrangement", *House and Garden* (November 1938), pp. 39, 91.

Vagg, Daphne. *Flowers for the Table.* London: The Anchor Press Ltd., 1983.

FOREWORD

Now I have read the manuscript of Mrs. Spry's book, I feel I am in the position of the Archbishop of Canterbury if he were asked to write a Foreword to the Bible; every word is gospel to me. The use of cut flowers standing in water for the internal decoration of the house does not go back further than the middle of the nineteenth century. From time immemorial blossoms have been scattered on the floor, beds, dining-tables for decorations and for their scent. Even in the early eighteen-eighties flowers were not all in water; the butler arranged trails of blossom, red flowers, geraniums, cactus, hibiscus, on the white table cloth. The manners and customs of good society regarded hot-house flowers alone to be sufficiently refined to grace the table.

Orchids were very popular. Indeed they are still very popular, though no cut flower lends itself less to decorative use than the orchid. Mrs. Spry does not mention an orchid. They stood in troughs of green-painted tin round a mirror carrying a glass handle; they were stuck into moss and lightly veiled with maidenhair fern. Joe Chamberlain's dinner parties in Princes Gardens were always arranged like this. In the summer the mantelpieces were turned into glorified window-boxes. Florists' shops sold buttonholes and were the rendezvous of gilded youth. In eighteen-eighty a show table was the vogue. A circular ebonized table in the Franco-Pompeian taste carried a glass plateau mounted on a grooved ebony ring. Over the whole was placed an immense glass shade which was made snug in the groove by a thread of chenille. The shade covered a collection of specimen glasses, with rare orchids, or the greenhouse roses Catherine Mermet, Niphetos, Maréchal Niel of which Mrs. Spry speaks with such affection.

It was left to Queen Alexandra, when Princess of Wales, to sweep all this away. With bated breath Sir Maurice Holzmann told us that the princess had large vases of 'common' beech boughs in the drawing-room of Marlborough House.

So we have progressed to the time when common garden flowers, chrysanthemums, daffodils, and sweet peas compose floral quincunxes in ten thousand neo-Tudor homes.

A new position has arisen which is disturbing to the more sensitive—the application of commercial methods for growing flowers for market, for example the use of a bunching ladder to ensure a uniform bunch brings standardization perilously near monotony. Sir Daniel Hall told me the other day that every lettuce in the United States has exactly the same taste and substance. So it is with flowers; there are more flower shops in London than ever before and each shop stocks the same flowers, in the same limited selection. This is where Mrs. Spry comes in. Her book pullulates with suggestions as to arrangements of flowers in the rhythms of the three meals and of marriage; and gives lists of flowers which run the gamut of architectural forms, and range from seakale gone to seed to the great white spider-lily of the tropics laden with the rich vanilla scent of Piver's shop in Paris. Mrs. Spry's job is to provide what the French call 'decor,' and so we find the flowers, the vase, and the background all interdependent. She is always on the look-out for out-of-the-way forms, and manhandles her flowering shrubs and berries. This is not, however, preciosity, but pure sagacity. Her insistence on the stripping of superfluous leaves was impressed on me many years ago, when I wanted scarlet berries in July. The aucuba, a baleful shrub which I associate with the Brontës, deprived of its hateful green leaves, spotted with yellow, supplied my need. When I say that the present practice in flower arrangement is on the level of English cooking, I have said it. Look at the lovely pictures in this book, let yourself be stirred by the text and your home life will be sublimated; you will be grateful to Mrs. Spry for precipitating an aesthetic renaissance.

WILLIAM LAWRENCE.

Burford, 1933.

FLOWER DECORATION

ILLUSTRATIONS

	PAGE
White Table Decoration with White China	122
Alabaster Bowl with Red Roses	123
Green Table Decoration with Fruit and Flowers	124
Shell of Nasturtiums	124
Wall Vase with Mixed Bunch	125
Alabaster on Black Stand with Mixed Bunch	126
Alabaster with Grapes and White Roses	127
'Chromatic'—Painting by Gluck	128
Black Bowl with Rhododendron Flower Heads	129
Low Alabaster Vase with Mixed Bunch	130
Celadon Bowl with Syringa Blossom	131
Black Marble Bowl with Double Syringa	132
Basket of Gourds	133
Seakale in Flower	134
Tall Glass Vase with Single White Rose, Laburnum Seeds, etc.	135
Warwick Vase with Green Love-lies-bleeding	136
Dracunculus in Glass Vase	137
Griffin with Dried Mixture	138
Copper Jug with Humea and Day Lilies	139
Pottery Vase with Rhubarb and Spurge	140
Stripped Elderberry	141
Corky Stem in Glass Cornucopia	142
Dead Group in Black Marble Vase	143
Stick of Longiflorum Lilies	144
Hand Spray of Arum Lilies	145
Hand Spray of White Camellias	146
Victorian Bouquet of Camellias	147
Artificial Christmas Tree	148
Formal Arums in Marble Vase	149
Group of Yellow Flowers and Fruit in Lead Vase	150
Grapes in Alabaster Vase with Black Base	151
Pink Shell with Tulips	152

CHAPTER I

INTRODUCTION

THERE are few houses in England to-day where flowers are not used for decorative purposes, for there is no form of decoration so varied, so refreshing, nor so pleasing to both simple and sophisticated tastes. Almost every one has flowers, and almost every one exercises care in their arrangement; but because of the infinite variety of material and the limitless scope for the expression of individual tastes, the last word is never said.

I have always found the most warm and heartening response to any suggestion for the use of flowers in an unusual way, and this is one reason why I venture to set out in the following chapters suggestions for decorations suited to various occasions and purposes.

This book is intended quite as much for the town- as for the country-dweller. People who live in towns for the greater part of the year derive especial pleasure from the flower arrangements in their houses. It is true that they depend for the most part on the florists' shops for their supply of flowers, and I have heard some bewail the limitations that they consider this dependence imposes, and envy the lot of those fortunates who possess gardens. As a gardener I deplore the lot of a town-dweller, but if I am to arrange flowers, I like to have behind me the resources of the most efficient of flower markets, supplied by innumerable growers who are always ready to take an intelligent interest in the fulfilling of unusual demands, with the advantage of being able to obtain flowers and leaves grown in countries and climates other than my own.

It is difficult for any one who has not possessed and ordered a garden to derive full benefit from the materials available in the shops, or to know what to look for. Interested people turn for guidance to books on flowers. So many of these are written for gardeners that they prove more tantalizing than helpful. I would like in the following pages to say something about flower arrangements which will interest those who have, and those who have not gardens, and although many of the flowers used in the decorations described are not what are usually regarded as florists' flowers, they are such as can be obtained with little trouble.

It would be outside the scope of this book to give cultural directions for the growing of flowers, but in the Appendix will be found a list of most of the subjects referred to with such brief information as may seem generally helpful.

In Chapters IV, V, VI, VII, and VIII I have given names of flowers which I consider to be especially beautiful and valuable for decorative purposes, but I hasten to point out with emphasis that these lists are neither comprehensive nor exhaustive, and that many flowers which are omitted will immediately occur to the minds of knowledgeable readers. This omission is not because the flowers have been overlooked, but because it would be impracticable to give any really complete list: and in deciding on which to include, while I have been guided mainly by my own personal taste and idiosyncrasies, I have deliberately excluded flowers that are unduly difficult to grow or too costly to obtain in this country.

My aim is to make suggestions which will help those who love flowers, but have no great knowledge of the variety of subjects at their disposal; to prompt others, whose knowledge is greater, to recall to their minds half-forgotten flowers, and to suggest the use of subjects hitherto unconsidered by them as suitable material.

In the hope of obtaining example and inspiration I have sought and read such books as I can find on the subject of Flower Decoration.

Modern bibliography on this subject is not large, and so far I have not been successful in getting very much help on that aspect of flower decoration which interests me, that is to say, on the use of flowers as part of the decorative scheme of modern houses rather than their display solely as individual objects of beauty.

The books written between fifty and eighty years ago are full of interest.

INTRODUCTION 3

Some of these old books are enchanting in their sentimentality and naïveté, and they introduce a highly moral flavour with their teachings in what they call 'Floriculture.'

From a practical point of view their advice, except when it is concerned with the culture of plants, is not of great use to-day, but their seriousness of purpose and the revealing light they throw on the ideals and tastes of their generation endear them to us. But they do more than charm and amuse, they throw into relief the difference underlying the ideals of decoration of their days and ours. It is interesting to note the frequency with which they devise elaborate schemes to hide the features of a room, and explain how some dull object may be embellished and adorned so as to be no longer recognizable for what it is.

Their intention seems to have been to conceal by an elaboration of ornament their houses, their furniture, and their persons. The following quotations will illustrate what I have in mind. One is from an excellent and useful handbook of the day:

> Ivy grows well in the shade, and may be employed for trailing around sofas or couches and rustic picture frames, positions in which its beauty is seen to the best advantage. . . . Where it is trained on the wall outside the window, a few long shoots can easily be introduced and trained over a neat arch inside, and its fresh green foliage will render the look-out much more beautiful by softening off the harsh angularities of the builder or architect.

Another is from an article called 'Floriculture of the Toilet':

> No fashionable lady can present herself respectably at a ball or an evening party without having a rose or a camellia in her breast. Let us hope that in a short time the crown and the bouquet will be rigorously enforced in every reunion which has pleasure for its object.

To-day we tend towards the use of ornament to reveal or emphasize the particular qualities or beauties of the thing we wish to decorate.

In spite of the fact that these old books deal with a form of decoration which may not please us nowadays, they have a colourful lavishness about them, a rigorous laying down of the laws of floral etiquette, and a definiteness of purpose which one misses in many of the later books.

In many cases the writers of more recent works are by way of being exponents of 'good taste.'

One school may be said to urge extreme aesthetic gentility. It advocates a sort of dewy simplicity in everything. Simple flowers simply arranged, one kind of 'blossom' at a time, and very few at that, nothing out of season, always a seasonable simplicity and no vulgar lavishness. The whole use of flowers is reduced to a series of rules.

These writers make frequent reference to the flower arrangements attributed to the Japanese, holding the view that if we would all follow faithfully in Japanese footsteps we need seek no further enlightenment in Flower Decoration. Beautiful as many Japanese arrangements are, and greatly as they must suit the background they find in their own country, I doubt if they are really suitable for us in England.

Another school of thought may be described as 'dainty.' Its watchword is 'lightness.' Ferns, trails of light greenery, gypsophila, grasses, and pastel colours are its indispensable concomitants. At the same time, illogically I feel, there is a good deal said about the 'natural' arrangement of flowers, that they may look as though they were growing. There is an echo here from an older book acclaiming the then modern ideas:

> Flowers are allowed to fall or recline on masses of verdure with all the grace and freedom of Nature herself.

These books belong to the time when small silver vases of flowers and fern were dotted about the drawing-room wherever a space among the photograph frames could be found for them; and in many restaurants to-day examples of this form of table decoration are, unfortunately, to be found.

Then there are books by eminent gardeners whose knowledge and love of flowers is so great that their views command respect, but it is natural that they should treat the subject from the point of view of displaying flowers rather than of decorating rooms.

So far I have failed to find books in which there is a general consideration of the use of flowers as a part of a whole scheme of decoration;

INTRODUCTION

using flowers as an artist would use colours, using them to stress the architectural qualities or the colour values in a room.

To-day there is a strong revival of interest in all forms of decoration, in houses, gardens, furniture, clothes, jewellery, in every form of beauty and adornment. Intelligent women of to-day take the most intense interest in the decoration and furnishing of their houses. Those who have no flair for clothes take care that they put themselves in the hands of those who have. In fact they show themselves efficient in ensuring, within their means, that their surroundings shall be beautiful, their tables exquisitely appointed, their food epicurean, their persons excellently groomed and clothed. But in this general trend towards a greater care and love of beauty and suitability, I think that flowers have lagged behind. There are still many people who regard flowers as necessities and no more. They like so many vases on the table, usually the same vases arranged in the same way, so many in the drawing-room in this place and that; in fact they order flowers and foliage once a week with the vegetables, and while they give much thought and care to other decorative details, and depute their clothes and their food to experts, they are apt to leave their flowers in the hands of those who are neither experts nor artists. They like flowers that last well, cost little, and are easy to arrange. Flowers may fulfill these qualifications and still be beautiful, but with the imposition of such limitations a wealth of beauty is lost.

I do not mean that flowers must be costly to be beautiful, not in the least, but if one counts first the cost, the lasting qualities, and the trouble to arrange them, and only after these the decorative quality or particular beauty of a flower, one cannot hope to achieve much.

The decorative quality must come first, whether it is a costly exotic or fragile flower, or a weed picked out of the hedgerow.

Some of the most exquisite flowers are the most fleeting, but I find that no reason for disregarding them; though as a set-off against such reckless spirit I would like to say that there are ways and means of prolonging the life and freshness of many flowers that are regarded as being too short-lived to be worth picking, and in a later chapter these are set out at some length.

In the following chapters I shall give an account of various arrangements of flowers that have been tried in many modern houses in London which have aimed at, and in some cases achieved, the ideal which I have in mind. I think the day is past when vases of flowers were considered as adjuncts to a room, but did not necessarily bear any relationship to the general decorative scheme; when, in other words, no room was considered complete without 'a nice vase of flowers,' small matter which vase or what flowers.

I repeat that our object to-day should be to reveal and emphasize particular qualities or beauties in our houses by using our flowers as an artist might use colours.

I know of a room where the predominating colour is almost verdigris green. It is unusual and striking, and not easy to decorate with flowers. A vase of magenta flowers, magenta be it noted, usually regarded as an impossibly difficult colour, gives an intense value to the green of the room.

In a white room an alcove or niche filled with a solid group of white lilies has the effect of a high light in a picture.

Using flowers in this way leads us to a treatment of them which is opposed to existing tradition. To-day, instead of adding leaves to our flower groups, we actually remove much of the foliage in order to allow the colour of the flower to predominate unmodified by the more subdued tone of the leaves—or we may remove the green leaves and add others which in themselves contribute to the colour effect we want.

As an example of the first case, let us suppose we wish to get a strong white note in a room, or part of a room, and elect to use white lilac or syringa. If we omit to take off the leaves we fail thereby to obtain the intense note required, for the green leaves detract from, and obscure, the solid white quality of the flowers of lilac and syringa, in fact they break up the composition into a series of patches, whereas without the disturbance of the leaves the massed flowers will give us the desired effect.

An illustration of the second case may be found in the use of brilliant autumn leaves (such as one finds in varieties of dogwood, berberis, and blackberry) and belladonna lilies; and another example, where seed heads, instead of foliage, are used—by putting together pink lilies

(*L. speciosum rubrum*), stripped of their leaves, and the seed plumes of spinach or sorrel when they have turned red. By this last combination one can stress the pink of the *rubrum* lilies in a most effective way.

Another result of our altered ideals is that we tend to concentrate our flowers into larger and more decorative effects. We may use an arrangement of bare branches whose beauty depends on outline and shadow, but no longer do we ornament our rooms with numbers of small silver or cut-crystal vases filled with flowers and fern; in short we no longer scatter indiscriminately and irrelevantly things beautiful in themselves but rendered meaningless by unsuitable treatment.

I am beset by a great fear that I may be guilty of the impertinence of being dogmatic or provocative about flowers. I think, therefore, it is best that I should say now, once and for all, that the suggestions given in these pages are offered with trepidation, and that if ever I sound a challenging or defiant note, it is in the hope of stirring up interest and argument in a subject which I think has languished, so that there may grow new ideas and efforts and thereby an increasing number of lovely ways of using flowers.

CHAPTER II

TABLE DECORATIONS

It would be amusing to collect the materials for a chapter on table decoration by adding to our own memories the recollection of our mothers and of our grandmothers, prevailing upon them to dip into the past to recall and describe to us some of the more glorious parties of their youth, and the table adornments most sought after and admired in those days. It might well be called the Rise and Fall of Damask.

It would be entertaining and mirth-provoking, it would also demonstrate in an unmistakable way the change in ideas and ideals which has taken place in the last fifty or sixty years.

There would be conjured up for us visions of tables triumphant with the doublest of damasks, the thick and gleaming table cloths, emblems of the laundress's art, bearing napkins like galleons in full sail, with serried ranks of sparkling crystal glasses, decanters, vases, *bonbonnières*, and perhaps arising from a large and handsome table centre an incredibly ornate crystal and silver epergne.

Table centres—these cannot be lightly passed by. The table centre was the heart of the whole decorative scheme. The red plush called for red geraniums or red sweet pea. The yellow satin trimmed with ribbon work looked best with yellow chrysanthemums, while the grass-green satin with pen-painted daisies, or the sheet of mirror painted with water lilies, might be used with more dainty flower arrangements.

Whatever we may think of these and other decorations of that day, we must admit that the matter was taken seriously when we read in a contemporary book that the *grand chic* was to have holes cut in the dining-table in order that the palms and ferns might appear to be growing through it, thus creating a 'tropical forest effect.'

In one house I knew the table centre on grand occasions was a length of crimson velvet bordered with gold bullion fringe; this was 'rucked' almost the length of the table and bespattered with small cut-glass vases filled with maidenhair fern and flowers from the greenhouse; 'hothouse flowers for the table.' Overhead was a fine and unnecessarily efficient gas chandelier with every incandescent mantle ablaze, no matter how hot the night, dazzling our eyes with the glitter of cut glass, the gleam of white damask, and the crash of red velvet, and as though to be in keeping with the general shine and gleam, the faces of the women were left severely free of powder.

All too clearly I remember the details of a decoration for a big dinner given during a shooting party many years ago.

My hostess had magnificent ideas about food, advisedly I say magnificent, and she was anxious that her table, of enormous proportions, should beat all records in the matter of decorations. She wanted to create a sensation.

We discussed the matter at length, visited the greenhouses several times, planned and argued and debated all the morning, and at length she left me and went to hold conclave with her butler. She returned saying that the whole matter was settled, she had had a grand idea which was to be a secret, and I was not to give so much as a look at the table till dinner-time when I should have a 'real surprise.' In this she said no more than the truth.

The gargantuan table, which stretched the length of a great dining-hall, was heaped down its centre with moss and heather, and on this lay dozens of slain partridges arranged with a sort of artistic sentimentality. I know she felt she had achieved a pleasant suitability in her decoration. The guests had shot partridge all day, we were eating partridge, and the table was decorated with partridge. Uniformity of purpose, what more could be said? Unconsciously she had even gone to the length of conforming to the canons of a well-known authority on flower decoration by arranging her partridges *en zigzag*.

The old books referred to in the Introduction advocate strongly the use of growing plants, especially palms and ferns, suggesting in some that the top of the plant only should be shown, the pot hidden by means of a hole in the table. I confess to a fellow-feeling for those reckless housewives who cut holes in their best and most expensive damask in order to obtain the effect they hankered for!

Around the emerging plant, fronds of fern were arranged, like a Fauntleroy collar, or the pots were hidden with coloured *jardinières*. There are pictures of three-tier stands filled with ferns and grasses and a very few flowers, and of small vases filled with tight bunches of flowers backed with fern. There is one picture of a wire arch covered with fern and pendent flowers erected over a large pot plant. All this sounds amusing nonsense, but some of the arrangements and materials advocated in these books have come into favour again, for example the Victorian posy, the close massing of flowers for brilliant effect, and the popularity of red geranium. Of all these I shall have more to say later.

A later book in the 'daintiness and lightness' tradition, says one kind of flower only should be used for tables, or at most allows the introduction of lily of the valley or gypsophila to 'lighten the whole,' urges dainty vases, delicate colours, forbids the use of such scented flowers as stephanotis and gardenia, abhors the use of red or magenta, and likes the table to be a bower of flowers.

I cannot think you can make rules about these things. One can only have an idea of what seems good and beautiful, and then use any means to achieve it. I do not like what are commonly regarded as 'dainty vases.' I love the scent of stephanotis and gardenia, and I do not want my table to be a bower of flowers, and I have found people who do not disagree with me.

All the books are agreed on one point—that table decorations should be low in stature in order to encourage general conversation, unite the table as it were into one genial whole; in the spirit of mischief I say that I can think of occasions when a hostess has been quite glad that her table has not been arranged like that; when the talk has been pleasantly intimate and agreeably personal and the flowers have not been in the least in the way. For some family gatherings I would advocate a perfect barricade of flowers!

Several books deplore the use of fruit as part of a decoration, on the ground that fruit and flowers should not be mixed, adding that it would embarrass guests to have to destroy the decoration in order to eat the fruit. It would embarrass the hostess too, since such arrangements are far from easy things to make, but when made they can be most lovely. So the wise hostess allows at need a part of the fruit for a decoration and arranges that her guests can have all the fruit they may wish without falling to on her table decoration.

It is one thing to argue about the ideas and suggestions of other people, and another to put one's own ideas into words, especially into such words as shall convey a picture of what one has in mind. It probably would be best to take hundreds of photographs and let them speak for themselves.

Constructive advice presents a real difficulty, because it is my belief that no general principle can be laid down for table decorations. In many books on the subject an attempt is made to formulate such principles, but I have not come across one which is not stultifying, or which has any general constructive value. The only way to deal with it, given your table and surroundings, is to use your imagination and create something which is appropriate and beautiful, and not to be limited by any preconceived idea.

The disappearance of damask, and with it the rigid convention of table arrangement, has led to the evolution of fresh ideas in every direction. Consider the table itself. What variety we have nowadays!—polished tables, glass tables in white, green, grey, or black glass, marble and onyx, the latter so translucent that it can be lighted from below in a most soft and pleasant way; gilt and gesso tables, wooden tables that are bleached or treated and painted in such a way that they look like fine lacquer—jade green, aquamarine, and scarlet lacquer. Some most lovely, some amusing, and all needing to be decorated with imagination.

There are cloths of old lace or needlework, satin, organdie, muslin or *lisse*, in cream or ecru, and many delicate colours as well as white.

Instead of sets of conventional glass, we use old goblets, or glass copied from classic examples, and glass of every colour; and we have necessarily revised our ideas as to what flowers and flower arrangements are suitable and in keeping.

The use of such tables and cloths and glass has led us back to the use of white flowers again. They do not look at their best on a white damask cloth, and so for a time have been used very little. Now they have come into their own again, and in describing some actual decorations I will start with white ones.

One was arranged in January. The flowers were massed in long shallow bowls. We used hyacinths, tulips, lilies of the valley, pure white cyclamen, white roses, and carnations. These flowers represent many gradations of white, and each has a definite and contrasting shape. Two or three flowers of each kind were kept together; it is usually a mistake to dot flowers about. Three or four cyclamen flowers, for instance, put together, gave a very white note in this group.

These flowers were on a dark and highly polished table which enhanced the quality of whiteness and added to the beauty of the flowers that of reflections. It was a fairly expensive arrangement, but it was used for three successive dinner-parties and needed very little replenishment. The hostess in this case considered that her flowers were as important as any other part of the preparations which she had made for her guests.

A similar arrangement later in the year was done with double white narcissus, carnations, roses, bridal wreath (*Francoa ramosa*), stephanotis, and what proved to be the *clou* of the whole scheme, the solid wax bells of lapageria. Now plants of lapageria are so precious, and the growth is such, that no gardener will cut more than the flower with the minute stem which attaches it to the main stem; and yet it was necessary to show the bells in proper position. So they were carefully attached to slim green stems from some other plant, and the joint hidden by the green caoutchouc used by florists. Once cut, these flowers last almost equally well out of water; at most they only require damp moss, so that there was no serious disadvantage in treating them thus. These, together with some sprays of a saxifrage known as Tumbling Waters, gave a fountain-like effect to the whole.

This decoration was actually arranged in pads of moss to last for one night only. It could have been done in any shallow vase or bowl, and would, of course, have lasted longer. The table was covered with a piece of old Italian lace, and the whole was indescribably beautiful.

Such arrangements as these could be carried out with less uncommon flowers and be quite as beautiful. A good mixture from a summer garden would be white Shirley poppies, roses, mallow, phlox, and white nigella, or earlier in the year sprays of syringa without its leaves, *Clematis montana*, violas, lilies of the valley, and garden pinks.

The illustration on page 122 shows a table decorated with white china and white flowers together. The flowers are short sprays of double syringa, arranged in an oval garland round the central piece of china, and continued in open circles round the end piece. Exactly the same arrangement was carried out with heads of lilac. The restraint of this decoration made it possible to have an additional adornment, that is, the decoration was not confined to the centre of the table only, but extended so as to include, as parts of the whole, individual flower pieces at each place. This is a good way to use old wineglasses, too precious for ordinary use, and perhaps too diverse in size and shape. The illustration shows stephanotis in small early English goblets, and gives only a vague idea of what a source of delight this combination of delicacy and fragrance can be. Jasmine is good used thus, gardenias, the separate heads of tuberoses, lapagerias, the heads of white begonias, and most lovely—white camellias.

Stephanotis is good, too, used in flat dishes or plates, and beautiful china may be used for this purpose because the starry delicacy of the flowers, sparingly used, need not eclipse the shape or ornament of the dish.

It may be said that it is unwise to show an illustration of a table decoration with china groups, since these are not to be had in every household; but there are often so many lovely things hidden away in cupboards, or only shown in cabinets, that I hope this may serve to remind people of their hidden and forgotten treasures. Old Staffordshire figures used in this way with less exotic flowers are suitable for a luncheon table.

The illustration on page 123 shows a chalice of roses arranged in a solid fashion and without leaves. This arrangement is effective carried out in white peonies, and later in the year in Frau Karl Druschki roses, or with heads of white lilac massed without green, solidly so that no stem shows.

I have read somewhere that if you wish to use water lilies, they should be given their 'natural surroundings,' a sort of pool created for them, with mossy banks, reeds, bulrushes perhaps. But if I do not want a rural scene on the table, must I be debarred from using such lovely flowers? The symmetry of their petals, apart from the texture, shape, and colour, gives them tremendous decorative value. I like them best in close formation, in low bowls or in chalices, arranged in a formal dome. In this way the whole character of their shape and colour is emphasized.

Water lilies have a way of closing up if they have been picked when just past their prime. It is entirely useless to pick them when the centres have begun to show a slight discoloration. In any case it is often necessary to open the outer green petals and sometimes the whole flower, to ensure their remaining open in the evening.

It is a change sometimes to have a green table decoration. The one illustrated, which is on page 124, is not easy to reproduce satisfactorily in a photograph because the shades and gradations of colour are lost. I would urge that it should be tried, because it never fails to give pleasure, and it lends itself to infinite variety of treatment. This one was made with the leaves of vegetable marrow and passion flower, a small green marrow, green tomatoes, figs, peas, poppy heads, water lilies, and the lovely marrow flowers, a seed-head of agapanthus and fruit of *Pyrus japonica*. The small berries are ivy without leaves. In spite of a certain solidity of arrangement, this group had a lively quality and lighted up well, and while it was not dainty it certainly was not dull.

Green *Iris tuberosa* arranged solidly with white camellias is a good green and white mixture, and green honesty with slim branches of snowberries is suitable for a luncheon table. The snowberry I have in mind is heavily weighted with clusters of white berries and is strikingly beautiful. It is referred to in more detail in another chapter.

Sometimes I put on the table a flat, thick, rectangular slab of glass, about one and a quarter inches thick, and slightly hollowed out. Although ultra-modern in feeling it does not look out of place on an old table. This can be heaped with bunches of green tomatoes picked out of doors, grey poppy heads, a few trails of love-lies-bleeding, and one or two sprays of tuberoses from the greenhouse.

There are many arrangements of mixed flowers which are good for the table, and here one may with advantage emulate the Victorians in their close packed bunches. One very amusing decorative arrangment is worth describing in detail. It happened in this way.

I was staying in a house where the flowers are done with great imagination and skill. It seemed to me that whatever flowers were used, or whatever scheme attempted, the results attained the highest degree of beauty and suitability. Imagine then my dismay when my hostess, who directed the arrangement of the flowers, asked me to do a dinner table for her.

I wandered round the garden in dejection. The flowers were lovely, but I could think of nothing that I felt would be a possible contribution to a house so filled with beauty. Fortunately for me there was another guest in the house who was interested, an artist whose appreciation of flowers makes her paint them superbly, but who disowns any knowledge of the practical side of flower arrangement. She thus brought to the matter a technically unbiased mind, and her eye was arrested only by what she regarded as intrinsically beautiful, without any regard to the earthly limitations imposed by vases, or the necessity of fixing stems in water. So I got a lesson not only in flower decoration, but in the emphatic necessity of keeping a mind clear of prejudice or fixed ideas.

Red cabbage leaves were the first contribution, followed by curly kale leaves, but only those which had turned slightly towards a yellowy green. These were arranged in two frills round a large shallow copper pan. Then came velvety begonia leaves, again arranged formally, and a ring of white scabious. After that came a mound of every lovely colour: verbenas, *Phlox decussata*, salvia, Bougainvillaea, zinnias, pale flame geraniums, gloxinias, purple carnations, and dahlias, mauve, yellow, and peach coloured. In the centre were yellow and orange African marigolds, and arranged at intervals were the heads of the amethyst thistle. That spate of flower-names conveys, I fear, very little, but by giving them I enable readers to try this decoration for themselves. It was really exciting, a thrill of colour, satisfying and lovely to a degree. It took a long time to do, because it involved lengthy and pleasant discussion about the shape and colour of every flower, but it was a great lesson.

There is one house[1] where I very often have to devise schemes of decoration for dinner-parties in a dining-room with old pine-panelled walls. This house abounds in beautiful things, and its owner is not debarred by preconceived ideas or prejudices from trying any and every sort of flower and fruit. She possesses many unusual vases and pieces of old china and glass, and she allows all and any of these things to be used to hold the flowers. On one occasion the cloth was of heavy soft satin, and to hold the flowers we selected three old china cabbages. When the lids of these were removed, the remaining cabbage leaves formed wide low bowls with uneven edges which enabled the flowers to be arranged without formality.

Iris susiana and *Magnolia soulangeana nigra* were the flowers chosen. This iris is fine in shape, and the petals are closely netted with delicate dark purple veins and look almost black; it is commonly known as the mourning iris.

The magnolia is a variety with large chalice-shaped flowers, purplish outside and creamy white within. The flowers were picked in bud a day or two before the party, and allowed to open in water so that they showed the thick creamy inner surface of their petals which lightened up the sombre grandeur of the *susiana*. Both these flowers have great architectural beauty which might have been dimmed by the addition of other less shapely flowers. They were fixed in wire netting and a few leaves twisted in and out of this wherever it needed to be hidden. This was necessary because neither the magnolia nor the iris had leaves, and it was important not to disturb the line of the arrangement by introducing

[1] This is the London house of Mrs. Somerset Maugham, who adds to her discriminating taste and judgment the charm of an open mind, so that to be allowed to discuss flower arrangements with her is a privilege for which I offer her many thanks.

TABLE DECORATIONS

foliage of any kind because it had dramatic quality as well as a certain stately and subdued beauty. In addition to the flowers, white china birds were arranged in pairs at intervals down the table.

For another party these cabbages were filled with a green tulip called *viridiflora*. Reference is made to this tulip in another chapter, but I should like to say something about it here. It has pointed petals of a good, clear green, slightly yellow at the edges. It opens out into a starry shape and has a slim and elegant stem which takes on pleasant curves after it has been in water for a time. It mixes very well with certain other flowers, but not with other tulips. It looks quite lovely with green and beige cymbidiums, and is one of the few flowers which do look well with orchids. On this occasion we used it with Solomon's seal. At first we tried the Solomon's seal with its leaves, but found that these eclipsed the character of the tulips. We took off the leaves, exposing the delicate green and white bells, and found the combination of the slim flowers and the star-shaped, delicately green tulips very good.

In the same room on another occasion we used white shell-shaped china vases and arranged formally in these the heads of arums, making a panache of flowers. This horizontal plume of flowers emphasized the curve of the shell. In the same vases we have also put white or pale-pink scented peonies, the heads massed together with no stem or leaf showing.

For a party in a white room in the same house we used a set of real shells, like very large pearly cockle-shells, and particularly suitable for small flowers. There is an illustration on page 124 showing one filled with nasturtiums. We filled them with masses of Roman hyacinths arranged in a sort of fringe emerging from the shells and drooping on to the tables. The shells were set in groups informally about the tables. In the centre of every table we put a large green leaf dish made of papier mâché. Each dish was heaped with fruit and flowers—green and black grapes, passion fruit, fresh lychees, plums and peaches—and among the fruit we put gardenias and white and purple hellebores. The grapes were raised from the centre of the dish and allowed to fall over the edges, the passion fruit was mounted into loose racemes by fastening its short stems on to a thin green twig, the purple hellebores emphasized the purple note of the passion fruit and the purple grapes, while the gardenias and green grapes lightened the whole.

At this stage, looking back over the suggestions, I wonder whether I lay myself open to the criticism that these decorations were in many cases carried out with rare or unusual materials, and therefore are of insufficient value to the majority. But I do not think so. After all they are only intended to fire the imagination, and readers will modify rather than emulate the arrangements suggested and find lovelier materials and vases and use them in more original and exciting ways.

In the chapters dealing with different-coloured flowers, I have made suggestions for various mixtures of colour and kind, and it would lead to unnecessary repetition if I set out in detail too many descriptions of table decorations. Given the general scheme of arrangement, one can adapt one's colours.

The foregoing descriptions are of arrangements for ordinary dinner tables. For banquets or supper tables at dances one has to modify these ideas. Height is needed, but height so managed that it does not obscure the guests in the former case, nor, in the latter, cause rebellion among those who are serving. This can be done by making a certain number of the flower groups very high, three or four feet if necessary, and using discretion in placing them. These can be supplemented by lower arrangements or by small individual vases of flowers for each guest.

For banquets it is as well to remember the nature of the guests. I have fallen into errors which have caused me great, though well-deserved, depression.

Do not, for a banquet for business men, evolve a subtle and delicate scheme of colour, or you may find it supplemented by a good strong bowl of marigolds or dahlias. This has happened to me. Men like red, and plenty of it, so turn your attention to red and do it well, and everybody will be satisfied. Flame, orange, and yellow will find favour, and a really gay mixture of colour is also suitable.

A modern writer on table decorations stresses an aspect of it that I find puzzling. He warns one of the danger of using colours that may ruin the effects of the women's gowns; he states that hostesses frequently send patterns of their gowns to those who are arranging the table flowers, and that what is good for the hostess is surely good enough for the guests. That seems to me to be subversive of the true spirit of hospitality if nothing else. But I remember once receiving a severe rebuke in a similar matter.

The occasion was a table-decorating competition in my schooldays. I had very few flowers at my disposal, but I managed to get some pink monthly roses, and these I obtained in plenty and used lavishly. I must admit that I added a few bows of pink ribbon. There was no doubt about the pinkness of that table. It won a prize, and I was accordingly elated, until a schoolmistress who inspired me with awe and respect, considering no doubt that unadulterated pride was bad for the young, addressed me in this manner: 'You have been awarded a prize for your table, I see, but I should like to point out to you that the guests at dinner-parties are usually of more mature age than you have yet attained, and your decoration would be trying to the complexions of most of one's guests. I hope in future you will show a greater consideration for the feelings of others in this respect.'

Gowns of the hostess, gowns of the guests, complexions of the young, the middle-aged and old . . . how can any one ever decorate a table and live?

Breakfast Tables

If the flowers on your dinner table have had that exotic note so desirable for an occasion, that high note of colour or shape which suggests a feast, they will be unsuitable for a breakfast table; to the extent that they achieved an exciting quality on the dinner table, they will be depressing at breakfast.

Breakfast tables are not really as easy as one feels they ought to be. Even the vases are a little difficult. Thin clear glass is useful and suitable for many flowers, but it is not always obtainable in the variety of shapes one would like. Old china mugs are good for some flowers.

I like to use vases and bowls of earthenware that have been given a coat of white distemper. These go well with most breakfast china, and they are refreshing to look at. They look particularly nice on table cloths of spotted muslin or organdie or of rough hand-woven linen.

Generally speaking, clear-cut, simple, and delicately scented flowers are best for breakfast table or tray.

A large whitened jar of pinks pleases many people. Of the white variety Mrs. Sinkins and Her Majesty are popular, but some of the smaller old-fashioned ones have a more spice-like scent. Also of the dianthus tribe, with the same clean fresh scent, we have sweet williams. I like the mixed old-fashioned colours with white eyes, or the dark velvety reds. These flowers look well in a large shallow bowl, massed together with short stems so that one looks down into the flowers. Used with their full length of stem they look rather ungainly and die quickly in town houses.

Of roses I would eschew 'florists'' varieties altogether for breakfast tables. A very beautiful arrangement can be made with that lovely old rose Gloire de Dijon; it has a new-washed look and a delicate tea scent. It flowers profusely, can be bought cheaply, and should be used in quantity. Take some in bud, some half opened, when it shows the strong formation of its petals, and some full-blown flowers; these will have begun to turn from cream to pink. Take off a number of leaves and arrange them as lavishly as you can afford in a big whitewashed bowl or in an old Leeds dish.

A mixed bunch of old-fashioned cabbage roses is a cause of pleasure and surprise to many people, but these are not easy to obtain in London, though they are definitely well worth growing.

An annual not commonly grown is *Dimorphotheca aurantiaca* and hybrids. It is like a marguerite in shape with slim and delicately pointed petals. It shuts up at night, and that is perhaps why it looks so fresh and wide-eyed in the morning. It is in shades of orange, yellow, buff, cream, and white. It is easy to grow and flowers profusely if the flowers are constantly cut.

As an alternative to flowers, bowls of sweet-scented leaves are delicious to smell and cool to see. The leaves of sweet geranium come to mind first. There is a particularly fragrant one called Attar of Roses. It is worth growing two or three varieties for the different shapes and scents, and perhaps one variety with variegated leaves to mix with the green ones. Lemon scented verbena, lemon scented thyme, southernwood or lad's love (*Artemesia Abrotanum*) are all good used alone or in mixture.

Luncheon Tables

For luncheon tables one has to hit a happy medium between the simplicity of the breakfast table and the exotic tendency of the dinner table, and as one has not to contend with the problem of artificial light it is possible to make many arrangements which would not be effective by candle light. Here is an opportunity to make good use of blue and mauve flowers, many of which light up so badly.

Among the earliest of the blue flowers are the chionodoxas. Massed in low bowls nothing can be more vividly blue, and if one has only a limited amount, they may be used in small wineglasses in combination with a piece of white china similar to that shown in the illustration on page 122. They are so blue that it is a pity to mix them with flowers more mauve in colour, as this detracts from their unusual intense blueness.

Blue primroses, either growing or cut, are good for luncheon tables. If they are grown well, they may be planted in shallow dishes. One can buy dishes with straight edges which look like stone, and on these the primroses are planted fairly thickly, and the surfaces and interstices filled with clean washed gravel or grey limestone chips; the latter are better.

If cut they may be arranged in small bunches surrounded by their own leaves. The bunches are put in small jars of water and then placed in a basket and the jars hidden by moss. A good kind of basket is a small garden trug or a hamper. Mixed polyanthus, violets, and wild daffodils may be done in the same way.

Another good blue flower is the grape hyacinth or muscari, but if you want it to be at its best for a particular day it is well to arrange it at least twenty-four hours beforehand, and in the country two days would not be too much, for it has a pleasant way of growing in water into delightful shapes. Its stems curve outwards and it assumes a sort of candelabrum shape. If you fail to do this you may find it a little stiff and unmanageable.

Anemones are popular for their bright colour and their lasting quality. On a very simple luncheon table I have seen them massed in a brown casserole. They looked well, but they look even better in a white-washed one, as do marigolds.

A flower which is popular with men, and is good for a man's luncheon party, is blue cornflower. Used solidly it is a fine colour. Do not mix with the other coloured cornflower, nor with fern or grass, just use it as solidly as possible to get the intense value of its blueness.

A mass of red geraniums in a whitewashed bowl is a surprisingly good luncheon table decoration. White geraniums surrounded by a frill of their own leaves are especially suitable for a polished table or a green lacquer one.

Nasturtiums with their own leaves arranged in a basket of moss or in a shell, as shown on page 124, are good. They have a quality of crispness peculiarly their own.

A mixture of pale blues which is perhaps easier for those who have a garden than for others, is of *Plumbago capensis*, ceanothus, Gloire de Versailles, and a few heads of agapanthus or a blue water-lily. The blue of plumbago is an uncommon colour in flowers. This fragile flower does not last long nor carry well, but it is worth using if possible and looks especially lovely on a green table.

A blue herbaceous phlox called *Laphamii* with veronica and the blue herbaceous geranium would make the nucleus of another blue group. These for a table adorned with blue Bristol glass would be uncommonly pleasing.

All sorts of odd things may be used for luncheon tables: little cacti arranged formally in whitewashed pots: as basket of moss with brown toadstools, red berries of lords-and-ladies (wild arum), small wild ferns and twigs of cones, and some sprays of a miniature tomato, with fruits, the size of a gooseberry, which grow in profusion and are bright red in colour.

This chapter threatens to become too categorical; I must not continue to enumerate subjects for table decorations. In later chapters, however, I discuss a variety of flowers, fruits, and vegetables which are good to use, and if they are read in conjunction with this chapter, the reader will, I think, find plenty of material for consideration.

CHAPTER III

THE MIXED BUNCH

It is a curious thing that, in spite of the superb examples set before us in the pictures of the great Flemish and Dutch painters, we are apt to neglect what I must call, for want of a better name, the mixed bunch.

These pictures show a lovely lavishness which we seem almost to have lost in our use of flowers and fruit to-day. The inspired and inspiring loveliness of a group painted by Van Huysum or de Heem is not only wonderful because of the greatness and beauty of the painting, but also because of the greatness and beauty of the thing painted. It is out of reach of ordinary mortals to paint a group of flowers such as did these old masters, but it is not out of our reach to arrange a group of real flowers and fruit such as they might have chosen to paint.

We must have forgotten about them; how else could we be satisfied with the flowers in so many of our houses, even when we have quite adequate gardens?

For how long have we seen, and shall we see, *tame* vases of flowers? Dainty is the word usually accorded. Sweet peas and gypsophila, Iceland poppies and grasses, carnations and asparagus fern . . . the changes are rung throughout the summer, apparently with complete satisfaction. It is not that these flowers are not beautiful in themselves, but that there is a sameness in the treatment of them, a lack of inspiration. The arrangements were not planned in a thrill of excitement, and they do not create such a thrill in the beholder. That may sound an exaggerated point of view to take, but is it? Do you not hold your breath with pleasure when you suddenly see something beautiful—a person, a picture, or a landscape?

De Heem must have felt that thrill at the loveliness of some group of flowers and fruit, or he would not have painted 'Fruit with a Glass of Flowers.'

THE MIXED BUNCH

Not only have we more flowers to choose from nowadays, but far more people have them. In many homes it would almost be safe to say that flowers are the only really beautiful things. It may be that here lies the reason of what I am trying to say. Perhaps we have come to treat flowers casually because they are no longer difficult to come by.

With such pictures to inspire, it ought not to be necessary to make a plea for the 'mixed bunch,' but there is a sort of prejudice against it. I remember once suggesting such a decoration for a panelled room containing some rare William and Mary furniture. The extremely knowledgeable man who was responsible for the arrangement of this room was obviously not happy about the suggestion. I am sure he was visualizing the weedy sort of collection one sometimes sees, a stem of golden rod, a brown chrysanthemum, a carnation, a bit of fern, a phlox, and perhaps a sweet pea or two; just a mixture without rhyme or reason. He felt he would be safer with a bunch of good carnations or long-stemmed roses, but in the end he gave way, and was more than gracious in his expression of pleasure at the result.

Over and over again one has to persuade and cajole before one is allowed to use a mixed bunch. But full of the true missionary spirit (or it may be merely of common wilfulness) I persist, and sooner or later the mixed bunch is tried, and then the contest is over.

One can see what disturbs the mind of the reluctant. They are afraid that one might put a country bunch in a sophisticated room, or an aesthetic mixture which just misses the mark in an especially elegant one.

We have passed through a phase which took pleasure in, shall we say, black bowls of orange marigolds, or pewter mugs of antirrhinums, or copper pots of gaillardias; all perhaps pleasant rather than exciting, and limited in a way that 'Fruit with a Glass of Flowers' was not limited. For a good mixed group it is very necessary to mix your flowers well. A dozen different *kinds* of flowers, apart from variation in colour and development, are none too many; and do not be afraid of mixing your colour. Be as daring as you like, you will seldom find you have chosen too strong a colour, rather the other way; you are far more likely to be looking for stronger and brighter colours than you thought to use at first.

The same advice is offered about shape. You will want solid as well as slim flowers, heavy as well as light, long and short, and you will be greatly helped if you can get branches of blossom, or better still branches of fruit, as well as flowers from the perennial and annual borders, from the various flowering shrubs, and from the greenhouse.

Take flowers that you would not think of using in the ordinary way. A trail of nasturtium, a geranium, some jasmine, a branch of acorns or loganberry, a well-shaped thistle, a stem of small half-ripe tomatoes or red currants. It would be entirely useless to try to indicate a tithe of the things to be used; I really cannot think of anything that could not be used in one mixture or another.

It is a good game to walk round the garden challenging oneself, that is to say, choosing subjects beautiful in themselves but not apparently suitable for use in vases, and picturing how they might be used. I have learned about cabbages and curly kale, but so far turnip tops and spring greens have defeated me.

The description of one or two groups will cause the mind of the sympathetic reader to leap to a dozen other possible arrangements.

One of the best can be made in the late spring. Branches of blossom, perhaps prunus or pyrus or lilac to give height. The lovely crown imperial (*Fritillaria imperialis*) is so often seen in old flower pictures that I need not urge its value. Arums, *Lilium longiflorum*, and tulips give solidity, and so perhaps does a stem of amaryllis. Then one may add ixias, Spanish bluebells, iris, stocks, and another flower loved by those flower painters, the parrot tulip.

It is best not to use too many of any one kind of flower, and to use the colours in masses. In this group red ixias and bluebells would best be used in bunches of five or six blooms; used singly you would get a spiky effect and you would lose the value of their colour. The amaryllis or an arum could be used low in the front of the vase, to solidify the whole effect.

I cannot emphasize too strongly the need for some flowers of a massive type. Without them the group is not satisfying. The study of a group by Van Huysum or de Heem will make this point better than any words I can find. Large double poppies, cabbage roses, peonies, tulips, and iris give body to their groups, and mixed with them are marguerites, honeysuckle, jasmine, larkspur, and spikes of corn.

Here is a good June mixture. Peonies, rhododendrons with the leaves taken off, *Euphorbia Wulfenii* (green spurge), the mourning iris (*susiana*), eremuri, Bougainvillaea, fuchsia, yellow arums, and allium. Some of these flowers sound a little 'special,' but most of them are not difficult to grow.

The illustration on page 125 shows a mixed group of summer flowers, mostly from the garden; the amaryllis in the centre and the Bougainvillaea on the left are of course from the greenhouse. White swan and purple poppies, zinnias, dahlias, *Phlox Drummondii*, red love-lies-bleeding, delphiniums, buddleia, damsons, *Lilium rubrum* and *longiflorum*, roses (Frau Karl and Butterfly), nasturtium, lupin, herbaceous phlox—all these in varying shades of colour made an effective group. It was a large vase and a large group, and it took up a good deal of space. It also needed plenty of flowers, and had it been so placed that it could be seen from any angle it would have taken a good many more. As it was in a wall vase one only had to consider a front view.

Such a decoration is obviously only suitable for a large room, but in the next illustration, shown on page 126, we have a miniature mixed bunch. This vase stands about seven or eight inches high, and the whole arrangement not more than sixteen inches. The following flowers and berries were used: scabious, *Phlox Drummondii*, zinnia, globe thistle, petunias, *rubrum* lily, nasturtium, fuchsias, ivy leaf geranium, lavender, asparagus seed, snowberry, white love-lies-bleeding, Japanese anemone, asphodel, and poppies. These last were of the large double varieties in pink and white but were dwarfed by the drought and though good in form and colour were very small, as one may guess if one compares them with the petunias or scabious in the picture.

Such a group has all the quality of a big mixed group, and may be used, by reason of its size, more generally. It is suitable for a small room—it is also suitable for use in a big room for a subsidiary decoration. Small vases are sometimes out of place in such rooms, but an arrangement which is large in feeling may have enough character to be used anywhere. Another example of this may be seen in the illustration, on page 127, which shows grapes and damsons, roses and carnations in a marble *tazza* about ten inches high.

The Victorians loved another form of mixed bunch, close packed flowers arranged in colours, a parterre of flowers as it were; and many such lovely arrangements can be made. Curiously enough they very often look extremely suitable in ultra-modern rooms. One can buy nowadays shallow rectangular glass tanks which are suited to these mixtures. In these, one can use many small flowers which are not always easy to arrange: aubrietias, rock pinks, wild strawberries, violets, crocuses, pansies, alyssums, gentians, sternbergia, and the short-stemmed green and purple wild arums. The same principles apply as in the big bunches; use strong colours, and mix them well. The Victorians often liked to have the colours arranged in bands, and for this purpose such flowers as sweet william, cornflower, candytuft, achillea, and pinks are suited. One often sees in florists' shops baskets of flowers arranged in this way. Close-packed heads of flowers are wired and set into damp moss and last quite well for two or three days. They depend for their beauty on their colour and the precision of the arrangement.

In the autumn there are endless varieties of berries to use in mixtures: hips and haws, cotoneasters, crataegus, the seed-heads of wild arum and deadly nightshade, ripe elderberries and blackberries; but a few twigs of larger fruits are needed to give character to the group. For this purpose one may use crab-apples, small, brightly coloured pears or quinces, or sprays of tomatoes. These last need to be wired or tied to a slim green stick or they are too heavy to arrange satisfactorily. All these look well together. It is best to take off any green leaves and to add a few autumn-coloured ones.

So far I have discussed groups in which both colours and flowers are mixed: another and perhaps more popular arrangement is the use of different flowers in contrasting tones of one colour. This sometimes enables one to use effectively flowers which by themselves are not pre-eminently suited for decoration, and to include in such groups one or two odd or rare flowers which are not available in quantity. Take for example a yellow group in which one uses the following flowers: tulips, roses, trollius, azalea, yellow arums, tritonia, streptosolon, and clivia. Of tulips I would choose the lily-flowered *retroflexa* with pointed recurving petals of pale yellow, or the sweet-scented Miss Willmott. Golden Ophelia roses last several days and open well in water. Trollius can be had in both pale and deep yellow, azalea in many shades of yellow and flame. One or two blooms of yellow arum and a stem of clivia give solidity. The variety of tritonia, King of Orange, is a good colour, and so is the streptosolon. This flower is best used straight from the greenhouse; it does not carry very well, but its colour is useful and it lasts two or three days if it has not to travel. The effect of such a mixture is a warm and glowing bowl of flowers.

In early spring and summer there are plenty of ordinary flowers to form bases for other groups. One would have the scented yellow tree-lupin, yellow flag-iris, the lovely little *Lilium tenuifolium* and the sweet smelling day-lily. Later still the invaluable yarrow called *Achillea filipendula*, pale and deep yellow marigolds, large French marigolds, garden roses, and sunflowers.

For blue groups one is more limited, especially if one wants real blues rather than mauvy blues. I have made one or two suggestions in the chapter on table decorations, but here is a suggestion for a taller vase: *Meconopsis Baileyi*, agapanthus, delphinium, blue thistle, *Veronica spicata*, larkspur, *Anchusa italica* (Lissadell) and ceanothus, and if one wishes to introduce mauves one could add clematis, campanula, and buddleia, branches of nearly ripe damsons and plums, the purple berries of the common berberis, and trails of outdoor purple grapes.

In other chapters I have made suggestions for groups of red, of green, and of white.

It is almost as impossible to refrain from being categorical as it is to be categorically complete. Every arrangement or combination of flowers that one may remember or imagine seems to stir up further ideas, and this is a very pleasant thought, because it means there is unlimited scope for individual taste and an opportunity of expression for those with the smallest of gardens and most limited means.

CHAPTER IV

WHITE FLOWERS

For some years there has been a prejudice in the minds of many people against the use of white flowers for decorations. Indeed this feeling has extended beyond flowers. White has been considered cold, unbecoming, hard, funereal, unpractical, and many other unpleasing things. Now at last this prejudice shows signs of dying rapidly, and though it may be years before we can get back again in quantity many lovely flowers that have been neglected, there is an increasing number of people who appreciate the extreme beauty of white flowers, and this will ensure fresh activity on the part of the growers in producing them.

White flowers are perhaps better in rooms of delicate rather than strong colouring, and I think are quite at their best in white rooms. If I could choose a background for them, with the sole purpose of setting forth their intrinsic beauty, I should have a whitewashed wall. Against this background the subtle gradations of colour are clearly seen. The variation in the texture of petals is one of the chief delights of white flowers, and this delicate beauty should be considered in arranging and placing them.

The petals of lilies, of magnolias, and of certain tulips have a solidity and texture for which there is no adequate simile. One has heard marble, velvet, flesh, wax, all tried, and all fall entirely short. Poppies and mallows can be translucent in their silky fineness, and roses, pinks, and camellias have yet another texture. It is in the interplay of light and shade, colour and shape in a thousand variations, that the delight of white flowers lies. It is subtle and distinct, cool yet brilliant, and is a matter for endless experiment and pleasure.

This interplay and these variations are not easy to demonstrate in any ordinary illustration, and I am therefore especially indebted to Gluck for her permission to use a reproduction of her picture, 'Chromatic,' the illustration of which will be found on page 128. Her painting of this group exemplifies the delicacy and the strength, the subtleties and the grandeur of white flowers. It has another point of interest to those who admire the paintings of the old Flemish masters, since here we have a modern artist painting flowers in a spacious and decorative manner, but with the same delicate precision and feeling that characterized the work of these men.

In a group of mixed white flowers the need for a few of outstanding shape is especially necessary for the definition, character, and solidity of the whole. These were supplied in Gluck's painting by the anthurium and amaryllis. The group, which is illustrated on page 130, is arranged in a plain white alabaster vase and contains peonies, Frau Karl Druschki roses, foxgloves, *Lilium longiflorum* and *regale*, syringa, and white anthurium. This last is more commonly known in its red form, but the white one is so beautiful in texture, and so lovely in form and colour, that it is worth taking pains to acquire. This arrangement was made in July when white flowers are plentiful, and many variations of it might be tried.

The value of white rhododendron as a cut flower, especially of the early varieties, is not always appreciated. The illustration given on page 129 shows them in a black marble bowl; all the leaves have been removed and the flower heads massed together. Treated in this way they may be used for table decoration, in fine glass bowls, in slim glasses, in fact in any way suitable for delicate flowers.

The illustration which appears on page 131 is of philadelphus (syringa) in a celadon bowl. It will be seen that all the leaves are off, and the ethereal beauty of the flowers on the slim, pale-brown stems is revealed. With their leaves they looked a rather clumsy bunch of herbage. They were soaked in pails for an hour or two before being arranged, and the stems were split for one or two inches, the thicker ones were also scraped to allow them to absorb water more readily. They lasted three or four days; with their leaves they would not have lasted so long. You will notice I said 'pails.' It took quite two small pails full, before the

FLOWER DECORATION

leaves were off, to fill this vase, but what does that matter when in the result you have one of the loveliest of all decorations.

A double variety of philadelphus arranged in a black marble bowl and illustrated on page 132 is a good example of a group which could be used to get that high light in a room which was spoken of in Chapter I; it had a dramatic quality.

I feel that in advocating the practice of removing the leaves from certain flowers before using them for decoration I risk criticism from those who think that flowers should be kept as nature made them, and although I think the illustrations may serve as an adequate defence, I would like to put forward one more argument. In the depths of winter most flower lovers dream of the joys of the summer garden. One may get a perfect nostalgia for the sight and scent of a lilac-tree in bloom, and one thinks of it as a great plume of scented flowers. When the time of flowering comes at last and you pick a bunch of it and put it in water just as it comes from the bush, does it not fall short of your winter dream of what lilac should be? If I am right and this has been your experience, then try picking a great deal more lilac and taking off the leaves, fill your vases very full of the branches of flowers, and you will recapture the spirit of your dream of a lilac-tree. If this pleases you, try the same experiment with crab-apple and cherry blossom and I think you will agree that the effect you get is far from artificial. Nature is lavish in her general effects, and you will also achieve a lavish effect.

There are, of course, flowers which possess in themselves a dramatic quality of whiteness and which have leaves that serve to emphasize this quality. Magnolias look best with their own leaves, as do camellias, gloxinias, and gardenias.

In addition to the general decorative flower arrangements in a room, it is pleasant to find, in suitable places, what I may call intimate flowers. On a writing table or a low fireside table, the exquisiteness of one gardenia set in its leaves, a spray of stephanotis, or a white camellia is appreciated by discerning people.

In each chapter I have stressed the value of branches of berries and fruit, and although the number of white subjects for this purpose is

WHITE FLOWERS

limited, there are one or two of especial merit. One of the best of these is the snowberry (*Symphoricarpus*). To those who only know the common form rather sparsely furnished with berries the better varieties will be a source of surprise and pleasure. I have some which came from Aldenham House, called, I believe, *Symphoricarpus laevigatus*. The slim branches are bowed down with the weight of numbers of large wax-like berries. There are several good varieties listed by nurserymen, but do not be disappointed if for the first year or two the branches are rather short. In and after the third year, if the plants are reasonably treated, one may cut branches three feet long, covered throughout the length with their snow-white fruits.

The white form of pernettya is another good berry, and although this is more rare than the coloured forms, it is not difficult to grow and it comes into the flower market in limited quantities.

In the white ornamental gourds we have a great variety of shapes and sizes and grades of white. There is a slim, greenish-white, pear-shaped one which is very elegant. Another is creamy-white with a rough, noduled surface. I once used a trail of almost dead white gourds on their own rough stems in a narrow-necked heavy celadon vase. The oddly shaped fruits hung down the side of the vase, and the end of the trail with one or two fruits lay on the table. It was a curious decoration, but it suited the Chinese vase. The whole thing looked aloof and strange, but suitable and beautiful.

The simplest way of using gourds is to heap them up in a shallow bowl or basket as illustrated in the photograph on page 133. A few of their own leaves, which are very handsome, enhance a group, but these must have their stems in water, while the gourds should remain dry, so that it is necessary to hide small vessels amongst the gourds to hold the stems of the leaves. After the first frost there will be no more leaves available, and one may then use bay leaves or myrtle; the fruits themselves last all the winter. Old white china dishes of a trellis design are not difficult to find, and look lovely heaped with a variety of white gourds.

These decorative and greatly varying fruits are as simple to grow as vegetable marrows. They should be trained up fences or arches, or grown in swags along chains so that their leaves, which are rather like fig leaves, and the fruits set among them may be seen to advantage.

There is a white-berried form of mountain ash. Unfortunately it is rare and therefore available to few people. It is very beautiful, but the large heads of white berries need to be rigorously protected from the birds who will strip a tree if this precaution is not taken.

White currants on the other hand may be grown by every one, and they have a great decorative value as well as being so good to eat. One branch well covered with the long bunches of fruit will add greatly to the beauty of a large group of flowers.

Sometimes an arrangement of black and white flowers and berries may be used with good effect. For the black element we are chiefly dependent on berries, although there are one or two flowers of such a deep purple colour that they look almost black. One of the finest of these is *Iris susiana*, referred to in an earlier chapter. Then there is a form of *Ornithogalum* with a shiny black centre to its white flowers, and *Arum palestinum*, which is black inside and green outside.

Privet berries are beautiful and might be more generally cultivated and used. When well grown the heads as well as the individual berries are large and of a deep shiny black. An arrangement of these with white snowberries is good and lasts for some time.

From France we get a very fine black subject. This is the fruit of a palm-tree called chamaerops. It grows in enormous bunches, in shape it is like a gargantuan bunch of grapes, the individual berries are about the size of a black currant and very hard. The main stem is sometimes two or three inches thick and extremely tough. A large branch of these fruits is a magnificent sight but can only be fixed, on account of its great weight, into a very heavy vase. The branches may be broken up and the smaller sprays mounted on wires or twigs, for they last indefinitely without water. I have known a branch last a whole winter, be stored throughout the summer, and be used again the following winter, a little shrivelled but still effective. Owing to the great weight of this fruit its import to England is costly, and of late I have not seen it for sale in the market. I find, however, that it is worth paying the freight and the duty because of its unusually dramatic appearance and lasting quality.

One can only grow a limited number of flowers of each colour, and there are certain white flowers that should not be forgotten when one is choosing plants. The following list is an indication of a few white flowers that might be considered by those who have gardens as well as by others who buy flowers for the house.

Bulbs, Corms, and Tubers

Agapanthus. Many people have the blue form of this flower. The white variety is equally beautiful and the delicate flower-heads are borne on very long slender stems.

Cyclamen. 'Flowers like two butterflies with wings across each other's eyes.' In comparison with the enormous number of coloured varieties that are grown, the white cyclamen seems a neglected flower. It is more purely white than most white flowers and is unique in shape, and for these reasons is valuable in mixed white groups. It is good also alone with its own leaves. It needs to have its stems cut and plunged immediately in water and should be well soaked before being placed in a warm room.

Allium neapolitanum. Because the stem of this flower smells of garlic many people will not use it. This is a pity, for it is delicate and graceful and the long slender stems grow and curve, after they are cut and arranged, in a beautiful way. There is really no need to eschew it, because once it is arranged in water and left undisturbed the smell is not noticeable, and unless it were in very large quantities I believe it could be used for decoration in many ways without the smell being troublesome except during the time the stems are out of water or the flowers are being touched. It lasts well and is plentiful at a time when there are not too many white flowers. Both the cut flowers and the bulbs are inexpensive.

Colchicum. The white variety of this meadow saffron has many desirable qualities.

First of all its shape, like a great crocus, is architecturally beautiful.

Then its petals are fine and translucent in texture and when it opens them into a wide star-like cup its yellow anthers are shown and the whole beauty of the flower is startling. It does not carry well, it is far too delicate, but picked in bud and treated with care it will last some days in water.

Crinum Powelli album. In shape and growth this flower is rather like a belladonna lily. It flowers in July and August, a time when white flowers of this kind are not plentiful. It has dramatic quality, is elegant in shape, and has a delicate scent. It would have the same distinction in a mixed group as an amaryllis.

Eremurus himalaicus. The plantsmen frequently refer to the eremurus as a noble plant, and noble is a good word to apply to the stately stems six to eight feet high, clothed, in this case, with snow-white flowers, though the prominence and quantity of the deep yellow anthers detract a little from the pure whiteness of the flowers.

At one time one rarely saw this flower used in the house because it could only be had by those who grew it in their own gardens. Gradually, however, it is becoming available in the flower shops, and although it is fairly expensive it is not dear, because it lasts so long and a few spikes make a magnificent decoration.

Fritillaria meleagris alba. This graceful bell-shaped little flower is easily grown. It is a subject especially suitable for use in some small unusual vase or precious piece of old glass or china. It has the qualities of elegance and delicacy and is best used sparingly, and in such a way that the shape of its petals and the delicate way the bell hangs from the stem can be seen.

Hyacinthus (or *Galtonia*) *candicans* bears a four- or five-foot spike of twenty or thirty bells. It flowers in the summer and is lovely. It is useful for big decorations either alone or mixed with other flowers.

Lilies. There seems to be no excuse in a list of this kind for making reference to *Lilium candidum*. It is so well known, grown for centuries in nearly every cottage garden, and to be seen in so many old pictures of flowers. But by reason of its commonness and the fact that it suffers from a disease which has exterminated it in some gardens it may gradually be forgotten and superseded. This would be unbearable. The Madonna lily is exquisite in form and purity, in texture and scent. Its season is short, for it does not respond to forcing, but in the short weeks it is available, there is nothing more generously beautiful. The broad-petalled type is most usually grown, the bulbs come in quantity from northern France and there is a variety with long narrow petals and purplish-black stems called *peregrinum*.

Lilium Martagon album. The white Turk's-cap lily is another flower to be seen in old flower paintings. This, too, is an exquisite lily but is rarely seen in gardens to-day. When fully established it has four-foot spikes bearing numbers of its small reflexed wax-like flowers. It does not attain this height the first year of flowering, its first flower-spikes are often small and slim with very small flowers, but these have a delicacy and beauty of their own and I have used them in making a sort of miniature Dutch group. In all its forms the Martagon lily is a desirable flower. The white form is expensive, but it is so magnificent when well established that those who cannot buy the bulbs should exercise the necessary patience to grow it from seed.

Lilium giganteum. It is really hardly possible to avoid an access of superlatives in discussing this lily. I once bought from a grower some cut blooms, and had to take off part of their stems because they touched the ceiling of an ordinary room, and they had as many as twenty great flowers on a stem. They were used in a huge Chinese vase at the foot of a stone staircase for a party. After the party the hostess gave a stem each to some of her guests, who found it necessary to dismiss their cars and send for taxis which could be opened in order to carry home the lily. That they are magnificent is obvious, but they have other qualities. The beautiful heart-shaped leaves of pale shining green grow the full length of the stem to the first flower. The pale-green stem is very thick and tapers to the point where the last bud grows. The flowers are greenish at the outside base of the petals and have purplish throats.

This lily lasts for days as a cut flower, its grandeur is quite specially its own, and although it is huge it is not coarse.

Last year for the first time I planted it in my own garden. Knowing that it is a moist woodland lily, I did not expect a measure of success as I could only give it a north-facing shady border. I bought medium sized bulbs and did not expect flowers in the first year, but practically all the bulbs flowered well. Instead of growing eight feet high, however, they only attained four feet, and I am sure this was chiefly due to drought. As I wanted to cut some of the blooms and was afraid that by doing so I might damage the bulb, I wrote to Mr. Constable of Southborough and asked his advice. He replied that I certainly might cut the flowers because the bulbs of *Lilium giganteum* are monocarpic and do not flower twice. After flowering the bulb throws off a number of small bulbs which should be removed in October and grown on for flowering. I do not think that this is always clear from the flower catalogues.

Ornithogalum. The variety *arabicum* blooms in June; it grows eighteen inches high and has a glistening black centre. It is a striking flower and lasts well in water and is perhaps the most desirable flower of this family. *Nutans* is silvery-grey with a greenish tint at the back of the petals. It grows about twelve inches high and its delicacy makes it suitable for arrangement in small vases.

In the winter we get from South Africa quantities of a member of this family in the flower called chincherinchee, a creamy-white flower which comes in bud and lasts for many weeks in water. It is this lasting quality which makes it so valuable. It is best used in quantity so that one gets a pleasing creamy-white massed effect. This is very good in a bowl of celadon green or in an old china dish. It is worth the initial expense of buying a quantity of these flowers, for a bowl arranged in this way will look good for many weeks.

Tuberose. An exotic, deliciously scented, wax-like 'party' flower. One stem of this flower will give a delicate scent to a whole room, and one stem mixed in a white group will lend a note of distinction to the whole. It used to be the custom, and still is with some florists, to use only the heads of the flowers, wired, for buttonholes and shoulder sprays; but we are becoming more lavish and use its long, thickly-flowered stems whole for our decorations. The English-grown tuberose is fairly expensive, but it lasts a long time and the buds open in water. It is altogether so desirable that it is worth having even at the sacrifice of some other small luxury. The flowers that come over from abroad are not such a pure white as the English ones. They are cream coloured and have faintly flesh-pink buds, very lovely and very sweet scented, they last well and are less expensive than those grown over here.

Tulips. The cottage variety Carrara is, I think, the finest white tulip. The substance and texture of its petals and the length of its stem makes this a most valuable flower for cutting.

Annuals and Biennials. If one consults a good seed catalogue one finds a host of desirable white annuals and biennials and it is not necessary to make a long list here.

There are good white varieties of mallow, godetia, clarkia, larkspur, sweet sultan; of poppies, White Swan has fine double flowers and Ryder's Malmaison, snow-white, is beautiful. These must be picked in bud and the tips of the stems burnt, the flowers may then be soaked for a few hours and will last for several days.

Helichrysum. Everlasting flowers have had a revival in popular favour. I still, however, do not really like them arranged in variegated masses, but the white ones have a special value. In the late summer, autumn, and winter we make large groups of the seed-heads of flowers. These are discussed at some length in another chapter, but here I would say that the white helichrysum is a valuable addition to certain of these groups which are kept pale in colour.

They should be gathered before they are fully open and hung, in *thin* bunches, in a cool, dry place. If the bunches are too big the inside flowers become mouldy and useless.

Nigella. Damascena (alba), Miss Jekyll *(alba),* and *hispanica (alba)* are three forms of white love-in-a-mist. The complicated structure of the centre of these flowers defies description, but their delicacy makes them suitable for use in small precious vases as well as for larger groups, and their seed-pods are invaluable for the winter groups referred to elsewhere.

Perennials. Some of the most popular coloured perennials have white forms, not perhaps very frequently grown. There are several good forms of white delphinium of which *Moerheimii* is excellent, it has delicacy of form and colour which makes it an addition to a white group. Oriental poppies are valuable too: Mr. Barr sends out a good white variety. The ones called Silver Queen and Perry's Blush are best described as blush-white. The sweet rocket (*Hesperis matronalis*) has a double white form rarely seen in these days. It has the same delicious smell as the single, but is a more difficult plant to keep. It is apt to perish in severe winters, and one should keep a reserve stock of cuttings. I think Mrs. Earle refers to it in one of her books, saying how well it grew when it could tuck its roots into the muddy bank of a stream. Perhaps this is the secret of growing it well. It is worth striving after for its lovely smell alone. Sweet rockets give out their smell in the evening; the single variety does not last well when cut, but a group of it will make a whole garden delicious with its spicy, delicate perfume.

Hollyhock, pentstemon, heuchera, digitalis, peony, lathyrus (White Pearl), and many other white forms of popular perennial flowers might be grown for their unusual beauty and value for house decorations.

There is an illustration on page 134 of the flower of the ordinary seakale, which has considerable decorative value. In *Crambe cordifolia* we have a form of seakale grown for its decorative value. This plant grows six feet high and is rather like a giant gypsophila. It blooms in June or July and needs to be grown where it has ample space, for the panicles of flowers are very large and it looks best grown in mass.

Gypsophila. I lay myself open to furious criticism when I say that with one exception I think that gypsophila is best used by itself. It has been employed almost entirely to help in the arrangement of other flowers, and used thus it gives a fuzzy, messy effect that I personally do not like. The double variety arranged alone in a very large mass has decorative value in certain places. In a dark corner or used against a white wall in a large wall-vase or cornucopia it is effective. In a considerable degree it retains its form and colour if it is dried and kept for winter use, and it may then be used with pleasant effect in some of the mixtures of dried seed-pods with honesty and helichrysum, provided always that it does not overpower the group and take away its character and definition. I think, generally speaking, it is best used in large rather than in small groups.

Shrubs and Climbers. If I could only have one white-flowered shrub it would be a magnolia, and I should choose the variety *grandiflora*, for its great, white, scented chalices of flowers and its shiny, grand, green leaves. But it does not flower freely everywhere. In Surrey, on a wall, I have had it flowering freely in late summer and autumn, but in my present garden in Hertfordshire a large plant covering a wall of the house does not flower at all. I believe that *Magnolia grandiflora*, Exmouth variety, is better in that respect. The Yulan tree (*Magnolia conspicua*) is beautiful, it has white cup-shaped fragrant flowers which cover its bare branches in early April. The early flowered magnolias are often damaged by frost, but when the flowers escape this, they are a miracle of beauty at a time when there is nothing so grand and spectacular in the garden.

Magnolia parviflora and *Watsoni* have flatter flowers, more anemone-shaped which show a mass of crimson stamens. They flower in May and June.

Magnolia stellata blooms in April. The white star-like flowers cover the bare branches in great profusion. A small spray picked in bud will last for days in water. Many of the magnolias last well in water if cut in bud and not bruised, and grow in such beautiful shapes that one branch alone is often sufficient for a vase.

Viburnum Carlesii. For many years of my gardening life I lived in a place so remote that the flower shows of the Horticultural Society were only a name to me, and I relied on catalogues for descriptions of plants that did not grow in my own garden or others near to me. I had a fixed idea that a viburnum would be like the snowball-tree, and could not visualize the wax-like scented blooms of *Viburnum Carlesii*. Now I should like to grow this shrub in hundreds for its lovely scented blossoms, and some day I hope I really shall grow it in quantity, for it is no longer expensive, it is certainly hardy, and no one who knows it will deny that it is a treasure.

Buddleia. The white form of this shrub is more delicate in growth and in constitution than the better-known purple varieties. It needs south-west walls in mild counties or the shelter of a greenhouse. But it is a lovely, delicate thing and most valuable for groups of mixed white flowers.

Passion Flower. The white variety, Constance Elliott, needs a warm sunny wall where it grows with rapidity and flowers well. Although the open flowers do not last long when cut, its buds come out in water and it is a most decorative flower. It may be used in white mixtures, but it is particularly suitable for use in any rare or curiously beautiful vase. I have used it in Chinese vases, in rare or unusual glasses, and in small vases of rock crystal and rose quartz. In this last the whole arrangement looks hardly real, it is strange and exotic and beautiful.

Wistaria, or Glycine. The white form of this climber is less often grown than the mauve one. A well-grown plant on a house wall covered with bloom will fill a whole house with its lovely scent, and the blooms against an old wall are extremely beautiful. One may grow it in pots or in the open garden in bushes or standards. Grown in any way it is worth having.

Philadelphus, or Syringa, or Mock Orange. From the old-fashioned, small-flowered, sweet-scented species to all the wonderful modern hybrids like the large-flowered Avalanche and Monster, and the doubles like Boule d'Argent and Virginal, these are precious shrubs. Not precious because they are rare or difficult to grow, they are certainly not that, but precious because in all their forms, small- and large-flowered, tall- and dwarf-growing, they supply a great wealth of exquisite flowers. It would be useless here to try to describe all the varieties that one may buy so cheaply to-day. I only urge here that they should be grown where possible, or bought as cut flowers and used lavishly for the few weeks when they are available, for there are few flowers more exquisite. Some small measure of their beauty may be gauged from the photographs on pages 131 and 132.

Of other white shrubs I would recommend *Cydonia nivalis*, a white form of japonica. The single white tree peony, Countess Cadogan, white clematis, the white ribes (flowering currant) many of the shrubby spireas, nearly all white lilacs and white broom, and the white-stemmed rubus, called *biflorus*, which looks as though the canes had been whitewashed.

Greenhouse Flowers. White geraniums, pelargoniums, the *Niphetos* rose, *Francoa ramosa* (bridal wreath), white amaryllis, and anthurium are all worth growing, and one unusual white flower called *Pancratium fragrans*. I believe this is sometimes called the spider lily. It is strange, delicate, and sweetly scented. The flowers are in shape something like a short-cupped daffodil with long white filaments hanging from the flower.

There is one white greenhouse flower that I would always grow for decoration although it is not suitable for cutting, and that is the datura. A good specimen grown in a large pot or tub, carrying numbers of great pendent white bells, is a marvellous sight and the scent is beyond description. It will stand out of doors in a sheltered place for the summer months and might be used for this purpose in England far more than is commonly the case.

CHAPTER V

GREEN AND GREY

Now that so much care and thought are expended on interior decoration, one finds many rooms of definite character, the unity of purpose which inspired the designer having been achieved. There is an absence of disturbing notes, and one feels that one might be in danger of creating one, even with the most beautiful flowers. Some of these rooms are austere, others have an elusive, almost water-like quality. This may sound fantastic, but it is the only way I can describe the impression I get from them. Such rooms, in many cases, are not improved by the use of brightly coloured flowers. In some, even white flowers are not suitable. This is equally true of some dining-tables. Glass plates and dishes, both white and coloured, have come much into use lately, and one sees tables beautifully equipped with delicate green or white glass, and adorned with shimmering glass candelabra, the whole effect being of great lightness and delicacy. Nor is this table equipment reserved for those who can afford to spend considerable sums of money; glassware of all kinds is now well within the reach of the most modest purse.

Fortunately for the general richness of the world, there are still people who cherish and use the old glass collected by their forbears, and I think with perpetual pleasure of a table which gleams with the subdued light of Waterford glass; and of another with old green glass which probably came from the Low Countries. In these rooms and on these tables, I like to use green for decorations.

In the minds of many people, green in decoration is confined to the use of leaves. There are many lovely leaf arrangements, but there are others, not commonly used, which have form, colour, beauty, and variety in such a degree that they may be put to many uses which leaves would not fulfil.

The hedgerows, the vegetable garden, and the orchard are all good sources of supply; and you must prevail upon your gardener to revise his views about cutting down herbaceous plants after flowering. You will want the seed-heads of delphinium, lupin, tritoma, iris, and asphodel, first in their green stage and later when they are sere and brown. You will want the grey-green seeds of seakale flower, and the seeds of sorrel, rhubarb, green artichoke, and onion. These last are invaluable. In bud they are good in colour and shape, and when they develop they have large spherical heads of greyish-green. Many people know the value of alliums, a group of plants of the onion tribe of great use in the border and for cutting; but the careful gardener will not suffer the onion flower in the vegetable garden to remain unless it is specifically demanded. Then the fruit garden and orchard will contribute branches of gooseberry, raspberry, and currant, apple and quince, half-ripe damson and plum, and later medlars. All these may be taken without the depredation being too serious, for they all last a long time, and a little of each goes a long way. I think almost the most valuable of these is the quince. In all its varieties it has a ruggedness of growth and shape one does not easily find.

If it is in your mind, as it has often been in mine, that you will be a good deal happier on these predatory expeditions to the garden if you have converted the indulgent, but secretly scandalized, master of the house, may I offer one useful line of argument? You are at most taking a few ounces of the smaller fruits and little more of the larger ones. In any case the birds and wasps will take far more than that when the fruit is ripe, and anyhow you can buy better apples in the shops. Nine times out of ten this is true, but it needs to be used with caution. The argument is useful, if not logical, but it will not convince the mediocre gardener, who will have a lot of prejudice, and is conservative; the good gardener, however, always agrees.

A green group is particularly appreciated on hot days, and in late June or early July one would have plenty of material to make the experiment. One might start with the seed-pods of love-in-a-mist, and *Iris sibirica*, grey onion flowers and their long pointed buds, small green artichokes, the long, drooping flowers of the stinging nettle with the leaves removed, a stem of broad beans, and a few heavily fruited branches of green gooseberry, leaves of eucalyptus or one of the grey-leaved artemisias, and perhaps one vivid branch of red currants; the addition of this one note of red emphasizing the cool tones of the main green theme. In these fruits you have an excellent illustration of what I have said about the necessity of using one or two flowers or fruits with enough definition to give character to the whole.

Another basis for a green group is holly; the shiny green berries, stripped of all their leaves, clustered thickly on the stems, are full of character. With them may be put wild hemlock after it has flowered but before it turns brown, any bold and decorative seed-pods, and long trails of traveller's joy, the small wild clematis called Vitalba. This has greenish-white flowers but is most valuable for its feathery green seed-heads. Picked in long trails before it is so ripe that the seeds fall, it is extremely graceful. We may also add the green seed of honesty (*Lunaria biennis*). This last is generally used after the pods have been stripped of their outside layers and the satiny white membrane left, but it has great possibilities before stripping, for it is sometimes pale green or grey, sometimes tinged with purple.

The group which is shown on page 135 consists of seed-pods of lupins, laburnums, dock, the seed of a yellow asphodel, and the flowers of the sea-holly (*Eryngium giganteum*) in its green stage. The seed-head at the top left corner, which has a windswept effect, is the green flower of the sorrel grown as a vegetable; it is more solid than the wild sorrel, though that also might well be used. The semi-single white roses were very full-blown. This group was made in June.

In addition to seeds and fruits, we have many green and greenish-white flowers which are exceedingly beautiful. In March there is the green *Iris tuberosa*, sometimes called snakeshead. It has velvety black blotches on the petals, and is both curious and beautiful. This is lovely alone, in close masses, or arranged formally with white camellias. It is sweet-scented, lasts well, is easy to grow, and cheap to buy: but alas, I know at least one grower in the south who will have to give up growing it and revert to planting the more popular daffodils in its place because there is so little demand for it. I feel convinced that this is because it has not yet been recognized for what it is, a subtly decorative and beautiful subject.

Still less known is the green tulip *viridiflora* referred to in the chapter on table decoration. People are apt to think of green flowers as curious rather than beautiful. I do not find any virtue in mere curiousness, and this tulip is beautiful as well as uncommon. I have known it last a week in a London showroom. It is slightly double, and is good in all stages, in bud, half open and full-blown.

A little later, in June, we may have *Gladiolus tristis*; the flowers are cream-coloured shaded with green, they are about two feet in height on slender stems, and have a delicate scent.

There are several varieties of spurge with greenish-yellow flowers, but *Euphorbia Wulfenii* has true green flowers, large solid heads, rather the shape of phlox. It has glaucous evergreen foliage, and grows three feet high on thick characteristic stems. Apart from the flowers it has especial value in the winter. Although it is evergreen, the lower leaves fall off leaving a number of ridges in the thick milky stem. These ridges, the tuft of leaves at the top, and the tapering shape and curve of the stem give the effect of some unusual cactus or miniature palm, and I have used one or two stems in a severe vase with good effect. They need to be set against a plain background so that the beauty of the curving stems may be fully realized.

The illustration of green love-lies-bleeding, shown on page 136, shows clearly the characteristics of this flower. I call it green, and it is a very lovely shade of clear pale green, but it is listed as white by the seedsmen. It grows on tall strong stems, and is more suitable for cutting than as a garden decoration, because when growing the long, delicate, characteristic trails are partially hidden by the leaves which are coarse in character. It is a flower to grow, which it does with vigour and ease, and to buy when it can be found; and it can be used in a variety of ways and lasts for a very long time in water.

The green hellebore has an unpleasant smell, but provided it is not touched after it is put in water this is not evident, and it is a good shape and colour.

Guelder rose, before it is fully developed, is pale green, especially the flowers which come from Holland or France.

The flowers of the lime-tree are of delicate and unusual shape, but rarely used in decoration. The reason of this is probably that the branches have been picked and put in water just as they came from the tree, with the result that the leaves quickly drooped and the whole decoration was a failure. If the leaves are taken off so that the flowers are revealed, the effect is excellent. The delicately coloured pendent flowers have great decorative value, and last for some time in water. They are especially suitable in a green or pine-coloured room.

The long catkins of *Garrya elliptica*, produced in midwinter, are a pale greyish-green, and one may arrange them, by a judicious pruning of leaves and twigs, in a cascade formation which has a delicate beauty of a rather Chinese character. This is one of the most decorative of our winter shrubs.

Two most exciting green flowers I have reserved till the last—*Lilium nepalense* and *Ixia viridiflora*. The lily is rare at present, though I believe it will become less so in time. It is greenish-white in colour, with a purple throat. It grows three feet high, and flowers in June or July.

Mr. Constable sells both bulbs and seed, and at the moment I have a few tiny seedlings showing from a sowing made a month or two ago. So it may perhaps prove not too difficult to grow.

The green ixia is mentioned in these terms by Mrs. Loudon in her book, *The Ladies' Flower Garden of Ornamental Bulbous Plants*, written in 1841:

I think I never recollect being more charmed with a flower than I was when I saw this plant for the first time in the garden of the Messrs. Loddiges at Hackney. A row of bulbs of this species, which had been planted in a narrow border in front of one of the hot-houses, were in full blossom, and the peculiar and delicate hue of their flowers struck me forcibly. I have since frequently seen this species (as it is very hardy and flowers frequently), but it has always been with renewed admiration. It is indeed quite impossible to give a just idea of these beautiful flowers on paper; they must be seen growing to be properly appreciated.

I do not suggest that either of these flowers should be used in quantity by themselves, their value would lie in the quality they would give when placed in exactly the right way in a green group. In addition to the fruits that we take from the fruit garden, we may grow, for decorative purposes, the ornamental gourds. These vary in shape and colour; some are pear-shaped and some like rough small pumpkins, and several of them are green, or white striped with green. They may be heaped up in shallow dishes, or, if their attachment to the main stem is fortified with a piece of wire, they may be used in long trails. They mix well with green unripe tomatoes. The colour of green tomatoes is very beautiful; these can be picked in long sprays but are a little cumbersome to arrange and are best secured with wire to a twig or a thin green cane. They may be seen in the illustration of the green group for table decoration shown on page 124. Here they were used with a small green-striped marrow, some fruits of *Pyrus japonica*, poppy heads, and other fruits and seeds.

Arbutus berries, usually valued for their bright red colour, are pretty in the green stage. Very often they will ripen slowly in water, passing through yellowy greens to yellow and red; one thus has the advantage of enjoying the branches more thickly laden with fruit than is usually the case, for the birds destroy the beauty of arbutus at an early stage.

In the autumn and winter, France sends us some valuable contributions towards green decorations. We get branches of *Magnolia grandiflora*, bearing the ruggedly patterned fruits which, as they ripen, show their vivid orange seeds. We also get maclura, a strange and uncommon fruit; it is about the size of an orange, uneven in shape, and with a most curious surface, smoothly corrugated all over. The colour is a most lovely pale green, and it has a funny cool smell, rather like fresh water; it is exceedingly hard and heavy. We have to fasten it on to its branches, and it lasts for many weeks without shrivelling or decaying.

There are many plants which have beautiful grey and greyish-white leaves, such as the artemisias, *nutans* and *Stelleriana*; *Santolina incana* (lavender cotton) or white scented thyme, variegated geranium, funkias, and some forms of ivy.

Iris pallida aurea has an inconspicuous flower, but its leaves are broadly marked with cream.

Many a time I have picked these various attractive things, feeling that they could look beautiful arranged in a vase, but for years I failed to do anything with them that did not disappoint me, and this I am sure was because I always tried to mix them with coloured flowers, and in the result only succeeded in spoiling both flowers and leaves.

They are useful and lovely if used in grey and green mixtures in low bowls. One might use several varieties of grey leaves and scented variegated geranium, and add the seed-heads of poppies or the greyish flowers of arctotis.

An arrangement which I have found pleases is made of scented geranium, lemon verbena, lad's love (a very old-fashioned, sweet-smelling bush), rosemary, lavender, and various other grey leaves; the attraction of this lies chiefly in the aromatic scent.

It is in this way, to my mind, that one can best use ferns of every variety. I do not like ferns with flowers, and yet I think ferns in themselves extremely beautiful. For long enough they have remained untouched by me for house use, but now I take fronds of every kind of fern, provided they vary enough in tones of green, and add to them the whitest of the variegated ivy leaves, begonia leaves, and perhaps some very light and odd little flower such as a spray of polygonum—anything I can find, in fact, that helps in shape or colour or character. Maidenhair fern adds greatly to the charm of a group of this kind, but one must only take the older fronds and soak them in water before using them, and even then they do not last very long—indeed the only way in which this fern will last in a cut state for any length of time is when it is entirely submerged in water. It may be arranged in this way in clear glass tanks or fish bowls and makes an agreeable decoration for hot days.

The Palestine thistle (*Onopordon Salterii*) is a magnificent plant. It grows eight to ten feet high, and has large shapely greyish-white leaves which may be picked and used separately, or the whole stem may be cut and placed in water. In this case one needs a very large and heavy vase, for the stems are of considerable weight. It makes a fine decoration for a large hall, and is useful in the border because of its height and bold outline. It grows readily, and it is worth while to have plants grown in a border of flowers which are reserved for cutting.

The leaves of the ordinary seakale are a lovely colour—cool silvery-grey with a white bloom on them—and the flower is cream in colour. After these are over there are round green seeds. The illustration, shown on page 134, demonstrates their value from the point of view of shape. Both the leaves and flowers need to be well soaked, and the stems split, or they will die very quickly.

Whenever I can pick them or have them sent to me, I am always glad to have branches of trees covered with long grey lichen. I am told that lichen is a parasite, and that I show a decadent taste in using it; but it is extremely beautiful in colour and general effect, and on close inspection you will discover a lace-like design of incredible delicacy. A few branches in a marble vase may be used alone, but the addition of some green flowers of the garden onion make the group more spectacular. Any rather formal or solid white flower may be used with these branches; tuberose, white anthurium, small arums or white zinnias, or later in the year, white snowberries.

CHAPTER VI

RED AND PINK

ALL my life I have found red a difficult colour. I have not liked red clothes, red decorations, or red flowers, and I realize now with regret that I have been unseeing, for instead of trying conclusions with red and finding thereby new interest and pleasure, I have eschewed it and shown in fact a will to stupidity.

It is so obviously foolish to shut one's mind to anything: yet it is very easy to slip into the way of disregarding the beauty or interest of certain flowers and shapes and colours, and of dismissing things airily without considering their latent possibilities of decorative value.

I have made up my mind to guard against this mistake in future by making a perpetual challenge to myself. The danger is that in taking up a challenging attitude to oneself one is apt to degenerate into an argumentative and tiresome person. After a time this may happen. Someone will say: 'I do not like such and such a flower,' and perhaps one's first instinct will be to agree. Then immediately one will begin to think how that particular flower could be used in some special way—some arrangement for which its colour or shape or size would render it particularly valuable; and then one will suddenly begin to plead its cause, grow enthusiastic, and possibly thereby become irritating and didactic.

A year or two ago I should have limited my appreciation of red to a few flowers—perhaps dark-red roses, clear-red flax and velvety-red gloxinias, and in arranging them I should have exercised care in keeping one shade of red to one vase, and even to one room.

Now I am going to advocate an entirely revolutionary treatment of red flowers. Abandon all idea of being limited to different shades of the same colour, and mix together scarlet and crimson, vermilion, rose, and magenta. Add quite crude and strong shades of pink and reddish-purples, and you will achieve an effect, not harsh and clashing, but brilliant and alive. Above all things do not be sparing or afraid, and arrange your flowers so that the whole effect is of red and not red and green; in other words, keep the leaves in abeyance.

I once had to arrange a bouquet of flowers which, in a certain light, would pick up the colour of a guardsman's coat; not to match it exactly, but to create, in a rather dim light, the same vivid effect of colour. I started with carnations which appeared to me to match it exactly, but when a piece of the red cloth and the bouquet were both looked at from a little distance, the coat gave one a thrill of colour and the bouquet looked dead. So I started again, putting in some darker red, then lighter, then a strong pink, and then almost a magenta, and finally something grew which had the same quality as the guardsman's coat, and it contained what I may call all the crashing shades of red.

The question of when and where the use of red and pink flowers is particularly suitable is so much a matter of individual taste that there is not much that can usefully be said. I have used red successfully in an eggshell-blue room and in a red room, and red flowers of a magenta persuasion are good in green rooms. One particular instance remains in my memory with especial pleasure, and that was an arrangement of red flowers standing on an old red lacquer bureau. This was an example of the use of flowers to stress a particular characteristic of a room.

August is a good time to experiment with red. There will be dahlias in many reds and purples, pentstemons, snapdragons, *Phlox Drummondii*, geraniums in scarlet, flame, and pink, the invaluable zinnias, invaluable because you can get rich deep reds and also almost metallic pinks and magentas which cut through the softer reds and light up the whole. There will also be found the seed of the wild arum, and possibly ripe berries of the wild deadly nightshade. Of magenta colourings there are willow-herb (epilobium) and lythrum, and from the greenhouse Bougainvillaea and carnations.

Neither the Bougainvillaea nor the willow-herb looks well or lasts unless the leaves are removed. I think a great many people have admired willow-herb growing, especially if they have come upon it with the sun behind it so that the light shines through its fine silky petals. The first time I picked it and put it in water with all its bulky leaves and watched it die in an incredibly short space of time, I was disappointed. Then I tried taking off all its leaves and found it lasted reasonably well. I recommend this as a decoration in a whitewashed room, or better still in a green room or in a very pale-yellow room. A plain celadon green or a whitewashed vase is a good receptacle for it; and it looks at its best with a light behind it. Bougainvillaea lasts better if the whole of the stem and flowers are immersed in water for an hour or two before being used. It is an uncertain laster and cannot be relied on to stand for more than a few hours, especially if it has travelled, though sometimes it behaves in a contrary way and lasts three or four days.

There is an unusual and spectacular flower that would be the making of a red group towards the end of June. It is called *Arum Dracunculus*. The illustration which I give on page 136 will show that it is like a very large wild arum, and its colour is a grand deep purplish-red. The back of the spathe is green and the stem green, mottled with brown. At the same time of year one would have purple and red annual poppies, garden roses, verbenas, geraniums, carnations, agrostemma, and branches of red currants.

It would be tedious merely to enumerate the flowers which might go together to make various red groups, and I have said enough to make any flower-lovers think immediately of many other mixtures and combinations.

Some red flowers show to greatest advantage when arranged by themselves. A bowl of red roses, such as that shown in the illustration on page 123, seldom fails to give pleasure. They are garden roses of one variety in different stages of development so that the colour varies a little. There are no leaves showing and the effect is a velvety dome of red. A shallow dish may be heaped in this way, or a glass goblet. One needs a good many roses of course, but I suggest that it should be tried in June when roses are plentiful. The result is an intense wealth of colour and delicately scented air, the joint effect of which is exciting to the senses.

I think the best way to choose roses is to visit the nearest rose-grower and find out the varieties that do well in the locality. I would like, however, to say one thing about red roses. One is often advised to disregard certain varieties because they have a tendency to turn slightly purple as they develop. This, to my mind, is a reason for selecting rather than for rejecting them. A few of these purplish blooms among the dark-red ones lend value to the whole.

So far I have said little about pink flowers except concerning their use in mixed red groups, and I will not describe any special arrangements of them because I think it would be unnecessary. I propose instead to discuss certain individual red and pink flowers which I personally like and value, and for which my feeling is fortified by experience of their worth in decoration. In the following list I shall restrict myself to two categories; flowers which I find especially useful in decoration and therefore take steps to acquire either by growing them myself or by finding a source of supply, and others equally valuable but which are not very generally known. The list, which I will divide under the headings Bulbs, Corms, and Tubers; Annuals; Perennials; Shrubs; and Greenhouse plants; is not intended to be in any way exhaustive or even representative.

Bulbs, Corms, and Tubers

I would draw attention to four varieties of tulips: *Sirene*, Lord Carnarvon, *Clusiana*, and *Griegii*.

Sirene belongs to the lily-flowered group. It has long pointed satiny petals. The slim bud is of a deep pink which grows paler as the flower opens and spreads itself into a lovely star shape. It flowers in May just as readily as the more ordinary varieties of tulip, and the bulbs are inexpensive.

Lord Carnarvon is a tall, strong-stemmed May-flowering tulip. It is a fine variety and of especial value for use in large mixed groups. It comes into the flower-market in reasonable quantities, and is therefore easily obtainable. It lasts a long time in water.

The last two, *Clusiana* and *Griegii*, belong to the tulip species; the first is sometimes called the lady tulip. Its pointed bud is cherry coloured, and when it opens one sees the white inner side of the petals and the big purple blotch at the base. It is about nine inches high, needs a sheltered warm situation, and is not generally grown in very large numbers in England; but quantities of it come over from France and it is sold quite cheaply in the shops.

The brilliant *Griegii* is of vivid scarlet with a purplish-black blotch at the base of the petals. It is about nine inches high. This is too expensive to grow in any quantity for cutting, but occasionally it comes into Covent Garden. Even when offered for sale it is usually overlooked because its true beauty is not seen until it opens and shows its magnificence.

Another flower worth mention is primarily of use to those with gardens, for the flowers do not travel easily and are therefore not frequently offered for sale. This is the colchicum, or meadow saffron. There are one or two good pink varieties, mostly of a mauvish tint, while the deeper ones are wine-red. The large crocus-shaped blooms open wide in water and have an almost exotic look. A single bulb will bear masses of flowers, and if these are picked in bud and treated with care they last well in water and can be used in many delightful ways for decoration.

Lilium Krameri or *japonicum* is to my mind one of the most exquisite flowers that we grow. It is really shell-pink, like the inside of a tiny little delicate sea-shell. It is lovely in form and has a slim stem. It can be used alone or in delicate coloured mixtures, and I have sometimes put it with pieces of pink sorrel picked from the garden when the sorrel bed is in seed.

The colour of the ordinary Martagon lily I can best describe as a dirty pink, a pale purplish-rose; but do not let this description deter any one from growing it, or buying it when it can be found for sale. It gives character and quality to almost any mixture of flowers. It is lovely, for instance, mixed with blue agapanthus either for a room decoration or for a bouquet. It has been greatly appreciated in the past, as one can tell by the frequency with which it is found in old flower paintings. There is a rare variety of it called *Martagon dalmaticum*. This is a magnificent flower, dark shiny maroon in colour, growing to a height of five feet and bearing many blooms. Because it is rare it is naturally expensive and therefore it is not often available for cutting or for sale in the shops, but it can be grown from seed, and I know of no reason why those who have patience to wait for three years should not grow a supply of this lily.

Amaryllis Belladonna (the belladonna lily) is a sweet-scented, delicate pink flower which grows about twenty inches high and blooms in the autumn. It lasts well in water if picked in bud and is a valuable addition to mixed flower groups, or it can be arranged alone or with trails of coloured vine.

Annuals

An old-fashioned red annual that I grow in quantity for cutting is love-lies-bleeding. There is an illustration of the white (or green) variety which will serve to show its characteristics. It needs to be stripped of its leaves and is only suitable for a fairly large vase. It adds great interest to a mixed red group, and as is seen by the illustration can be effectively used alone.

An annual called ricinus has large, handsome reddish leaves which are not much use for cutting because they die so soon, but it bears bracts of lovely red fruits, like small chestnut burrs, quite lovely, both in shape and colour.

Poppies I regard as indispensable flowers, especially the large tall variety which can be had in many shades of pink and red. Ryder & Son, of St. Albans, offer a variety called Malmaison poppies. They are two and a half feet high and there are five or six shades of pink and red. Both these and Shirley poppies should be picked when the buds are just opening and the tips of the stems dipped into boiling water for a few seconds. If they are treated thus they carry and last well.

Larkspurs, stocks, godetia, and clarkia are all valuable summer flowers for cutting, as is lavatera, the annual tree mallow, which can be got in pink and rose. This is another flower that may be denuded of its leaves. The opened flowers bruise too easily for it to travel well, but the buds come out rapidly in water.

Perennials

Dielytra spectabilis (bleeding heart, or lady's locket—the last name describes it best) is an old-fashioned and very pretty pink flower. For a long time it was only to be seen in old-fashioned gardens, and then it was found that it forced readily and was therefore useful for early pot-plants, and now it is sold in quantities in pots in the early spring. The delicate bract of heart-shaped flowers is a good addition to a group of flowers.

One of the most spectacular of flowers is the eremurus, and the variety *Elwesianus* is a delicate shade of pink. This giant among flowers will last in water for many days, and lately has been coming into the flower-market. It is worth growing, and worth buying when one can find the blooms offered for sale.

Megasea is an early and effective rose-pink flower. One gets it in March and April, and its dense masses of flowers are valuable at that time of year, and from a gardener's point of view it has an added value in that its large, well-shaped leaves turn to brilliant colours in the autumn.

Of *Chrysanthemums* I will mention one variety only—Rayonnante. I like its spidery shape and its rather dull soft colour, and it lasts well and mixes with other flowers, which is not the case with many chrysanthemums.

Monarda didyma, or bergamot, is worth growing for its scent alone; sidalcea, lychnis, *Lobelia cardinalis,* canna, hollyhocks, and double and single peony, all are worth growing for cut flowers and worth buying when that is possible.

RED AND PINK

Shrubs

Rhododendrons. The illustration of white rhododendrons shows that by removing the leaves and using the flowers in a mass one can get good decorative effect. Pink or red rhododendrons treated in this way or used in mixed bunches are among the most useful of flowering shrubs.

Kalmia is a delightful evergreen shrub with waxy pink flowers which are of unusual shape in bud and flower.

Daphne Mezereum. I would like to wax lyrical about this lovely flower. It blooms so early, is so deliciously scented, and the short branches are covered thickly with the pinkish-mauve coloured flowers. In some gardens one may see an odd bush of it, but rarely is it grown in quantity and rarely picked. It is not expensive, it grows easily if its few cultural requirements are observed, and it lasts reasonably well in water.

Clematis montana rubens. This climber has pinkish flowers of the same shape as the white variety. One can pick long trails of it, and it carries and lasts quite well.

A pink variety of pampas grass, *grandiflorum roseum*, has long silky plumes of pale rose colour. Arranged with pink lilies or Rayonnante chrysanthemums, or in any mixture of pink autumn flowers, it makes an unusual and beautiful group.

I need not stress the value of the spring flowering trees of prunus and pyrus, nor of the innumerable berried shrubs in the autumn.

Camellias. We might take a leaf out of the Victorians' book about this flower, for a great many of the fine specimens we now have were planted by them. They loved this wax-like, shapely flower, red and pink, white and striped, double and single in its shiny green leaves. I do not know why, but it seems to me to be a party flower in spite of its sturdiness. It grows out of doors in sheltered gardens, and Mr. Norman Wilkinson grew it in quantity in an interesting and beautiful way in his garden at Chiswick. He had a simple glass structure built against a wall; it was not heated, and during the summer the doors and windows were wide open so that there was no greenhouse atmosphere. There he grew many varieties of camellia, some especially rare and beautiful.

So many flowers grown in or near London just live in a poor, half-hearted fashion, but these flowers flourish, showing that they are thoroughly happy and at home.

Roses. There are few pink flowers of greater charm than pink moss roses; there is something particularly fascinating and romantic about them. It is best to grow them in beds apart from other roses, and one wants them in fairly large quantity to be able to gather enough at one time to be effective. Another old-fashioned rose which seems to me to hold its own against new-comers is the La France rose—it is delicate in colour, good in shape, and deliciously scented, but although every one knows it by name and many people grow a few plants of it, it does not seem to be grown in really great quantity nowadays.

Greenhouse Flowers

Bougainvillaea—variety Mrs. Butt. This is a more rosy colour than the one usually grown, and more generally useful for cutting.

Amaryllis. One stem of amaryllis is such a valuable addition to a flower group that it is worth while growing even a small quantity. They are not difficult to grow, and they are truly magnificent flowers.

Anthuriums are regarded as rather strange and unreal looking flowers, and are sometimes described as looking as though they were made of American cloth. They are most commonly known in their brilliant red form. The white one shown in the illustration of the mixed group, on page 129, is not very common, and between this and the red there are various shades of pink. Some are white just flushed with pink, and others a lovely pale-rose colour. Those who can grow these flowers and who have confined themselves to the red variety would probably delight in these other colours.

Lapageria rosea is another greenhouse flower not commonly grown. The white variety is beautiful, but *rosea* is a deep rose-pink, very lovely, and it flowers freely.

And last, but most assuredly not least, geraniums. I cannot name all the greenhouse kinds I would like to have, nor hope to describe the subtle variations of colour in every shade of red and pink. The only advice I can offer is that the Royal Horticultural Show should be visited and the growers of geraniums sought out. You will probably fall at once for eight or ten different varieties; probably most of them will be true greenhouse varieties, and you will be disappointed if you fall into an error, not uncommon, of putting them out of doors with the ivy-leaves and Paul Crampels. They will not thrive thus. They only do really well in the greenhouse. A great mixed bunch of them is a lovely thing.

I have referred to the use of one or two fruits and berries which are needed to add solidity and character to groups of flowers. There is a variety of tomato which is most suitable for this purpose. It has small red fruits not much bigger than cherries. The fruits are borne in long drooping racemes, and are brilliant in colour. It is worth giving a little space for a few of these plants. They are grown sometimes for use in salads, but have greater value, I think, for decoration. They should be picked before they are very ripe, or some of the fruit will drop off the stems.

CHAPTER VII

YELLOW, GOLD, CREAM, AND BROWN

In recent years there has been a decline in the popularity of yellow for house decoration, and flowers of this colour seem also less in favour for use in the house than they were at one time.

There are obviously many exceptions to this feeling.

There are some flowers which, by reason of their shape and colour, or the way in which they grow, make an appeal to all lovers of beauty, and are sought and enjoyed by those who would not normally choose yellow flowers. On the other hand, there are some people who have a predilection in favour of yellow—so strong that they take little interest in any other flowers, and only depart from their favourite yellows and oranges into flame colour and terra cotta, or possibly the various salmon shades of pink.

This singleness of purpose seems to be a particular characteristic of lovers of this one range of colours; those of us who prefer others seem to have more catholic tastes or less single minds.

It may be purely fortuitous, but I have noticed that this strong bias is usually found in people of a certain complexion, the colouring of which often goes with golden or red hair, so possibly it is due to something deeper than an ordinarily acquired taste for colour. In either case, whether one loves yellow to the exclusion of other colours, or whether one prefers blues and pinks and greens with a very definite exception in favour of certain yellow flowers, one must recognize that in many mixed groups of colour yellow plays an important part.

In discussing the best backgrounds for white flowers, or for pink or green or blue, one seems to have a clearer idea of what would look best than one has in the case of yellow flowers, and this may be because there is less need for any special background. Would it be an exaggeration to say that yellow flowers will go almost everywhere but are not specially striking anywhere? Immediately I want to make an exception. Against a background of faded magenta brocade or old plum-coloured fabric probably nothing would look better than an arrangement of yellow flowers.

In dark rooms or dark corners yellow is especially useful. A room panelled in dark wood is a difficult background, and probably one would find that yellow flowers were more satisfactory than any others for its decoration.

In one London church where the walls are entirely green, I have found an arrangement of yellow, orange, and flame more effective than any other colouring.

Pre-eminent among flowers of special appeal are one or two lilies. *Lilium testaceum*, or the Nankeen lily, sometimes called *Isabellinum*, is an old inhabitant of English gardens, but not often seen nowadays. It has become rare and therefore expensive. It varies a little in colour according to the soil it grows in—from a warm buff, almost apricot, to a deeper shade of apricot.

I have seen it at its best in cottage gardens very far north; where it flourishes, its four-foot stems bear as many as ten or twelve of the reflexed flowers.

Another yellow lily, *L. monadelphum szovitzianum*, is also desirable and scarce. It has clear yellow flowers, spotted with black, rather bell-like in shape, growing on slender stems.

It may be a little tantalizing to mention lilies which are scarce and expensive, but one may grow them from seed, and they are well worth the patience that this requires.

Among spectacular flowers there are several good varieties of eremuri. *E. Bungei* is bright yellow, *E. Warei* buff yellow, and *E. Shelford* coppery yellow. All are good, and all of great value for big decorative effects—either used alone or as the main feature of a big group.

Of smaller flowers, the *Sternbergia lutea* is a treasure: this flower, were it not for its stem, might easily be taken for a crocus; but it grows on a short daffodil-like stem. It blooms in autumn and differs from a crocus in that it is less fragile and travels and lasts quite well. In some gardens it blooms profusely and regularly, and in others very sparsely. I believe the secret of its thriving is good drainage. I have it planted as a border to a narrow bed of belladonna lilies outside a greenhouse where the drainage is exceptionally good. It has been there for three years and has never failed to bloom.

We bring over from France branches of unripe persimmon fruits (sometimes called the Golden Apples of the Hesperides). When they arrive they are a lovely greyish-green in colour: as they ripen they pass through various shades of yellow to golden. The shape of the fruits and the way they grow on the pale-brown branches gives them a rather Chinese quality, and a branch of these wedged into a heavy vase looks strange and beautiful.

Chinese in effect also may be a well-shaped branch of laburnum which is stripped of all its leaves, and if the variety used is *Vossi* (which has very long racemes of pale flowers) the effect will be enhanced.

In the chapter on wedding flowers there is reference to mixed bouquets of yellow, orange, and flame-coloured flowers, and no good purpose would be served by describing a number of such here; later on, in the list at the end of the chapter, many flowers are mentioned which would be suitable for making yellow groups.

I had once to fill two large and very beautiful alabaster vases for a special occasion. It was in October. There were a few late dahlias and gladioli, roses and lilies, and of course plenty of chrysanthemums; but none of them seemed suitable for the purpose. The vases, classic in shape, old, and of a deep cream colour, were eventually filled with a mixture which I will describe in some detail, because variants of this particular arrangement have proved of value many times.

The whole effect was a deep cream and brown, and was obtained by using seed-heads and fruits and other materials which would usually be regarded as dead. In detail the group was composed of the seed-heads of wild hemlock, which varied from pale parchment colour to leaf brown, the pale-brown seeds of delphinium and the dry fronds of a shrubby spirea called *ariaefolia*, and one or two heads of *Hydrangea paniculata* which had turned quite brown on their stems but had retained their shape: branches of horse-chestnut and medlar were used, with the fruits but not the leaves. Among these seed and fruits we put the buff variety of the chrysanthemum Rayonnante, and last of all there were trails of hops. All the leaves were off, and the flowers had turned the palest faintest brown. They fell in a cascade, but thinly, so that the beauty of the vase was not eclipsed.

This arrangement can be varied in a hundred ways, and on page 143 there is an illustration of this kind. Here we have the spirea, hydrangea, delphinium, and medlar fruits, and in addition honesty, bocconia, lupin, yarrow, and eryngium. You may keep the whole tone rather pale in palish browns and dim grey-greens, or you may introduce colour by the use of helichrysums and statice, or that shapely yarrow called *Achillea Eupatorium*, and your group will still be composed of materials that will last for many months. It may be given temporary strong colour with autumn leaves and berries; blackberries and mulberries being particularly good.

The illustration on page 138 shows such a group of particularly pale tone. There is dried statice and teazle, honesty both with the seed-capsules stripped and unstripped, cream helichrysums, green and pale-cream gourds, and miscellaneous seed-pods, including a stem or two of *Bocconia cordata*. This plant, sometimes called plume poppy, is a cream-coloured flower with beautiful leaves of green and grey. When the flower has fallen there is a feathery, ghost-like remainder. The transparent leaves are the skeleton leaves of magnolia. These come from abroad, and may be purchased in England—but one might use any skeleton leaves such as are found under trees. They should be mounted carefully on branches suitable to the character of the leaf. The long tassels in the group are the flowers of green love-lies-bleeding dried; they are of a particularly good shade of pale greenish-buff. The red variety is brownish when dried and is suitable for a group of darker tone.

Larch cones, acorns, dried heads of golden rod, lupin seeds, and poppy heads are all good, and when once a group on these lines has been made, there will be no end to the ideas which suggest themselves.

Another arrangement which suits these same vases is of *auratum* lily and *Humea elegans*. This aromatic plant is sometimes called the incense plant. It is of value from many points of view. It is graceful, as will be apparent from the illustration on page 139; it has a lovely coppery colour, it lasts for a very long time when cut, and can be kept throughout the winter. Its scent fills the room and may remain long after the plant has been removed. In the picture it is shown with a copper-brown day-lily.

On another occasion we wanted to fill a large vase in a corner of an old pine room which had hangings of soft pale green and parchment, and these were the colours we sought to emphasize. The month was May, and though flowers were plentiful, there seemed at first nothing entirely suitable, until we found a quantity of rhubarb in flower. The great creamy plumes of this were exactly what was needed, and we added some big green heads of *Euphorbia Wulfenii*. There is an illustration of a smaller edition of this arrangement on page 140, but one cannot gain any real impression of the subtleties of colour, which had great charm, nor will words adequately describe how lovely those masses of cream and soft green looked.

There are several forms of cultivated rhubarb: *Rheum Alexandrae, R. tanghuticum*, and others, which are very fine plants and which should certainly be grown where there is space for them; but none is more beautiful in colour than the ordinary garden variety. It is, of course, the practice of the careful gardener to cut the flowering stems of rhubarb, as of seakale and sorrel; so one has to be judiciously explanatory, even obstinate on this score, or there would be none of these interesting things to be found in a well-kept garden.

Lately, motoring in Scotland, I found some very fine lichen-covered branches which I picked in quantity, and treated with care, but I fell sadly under suspicion, as I could tell by the surprised faces of several stately hall-porters who supervised the unloading of the luggage at subsequent hotels.

The illustration on page 141 shows a marble vase filled with elder flowers in different stages of development. Those in the middle of the picture are quite over, only the skeleton of the flower remains; some have the berries just forming. This is a good stage at which to pick elder, it lasts well; when in full flower it is not an easy matter to keep it for long unless one cuts the heads off and uses them massed in bowls.

Among cream flowers yucca is one of the giants. It has spikes of bell-shaped blossoms, maybe five or six feet high. It lasts well, and makes a fine decoration by itself. If mixed with other flowers its cream colour is emphasized and thrown into relief by the use of pale browns and buffs.

So far I have only suggested rather large forms of cream and brown decorations. Among the smaller ones, a bowl of tulip Safrano (or Tea Rose) is good. It is described as pale yellow, flushed with salmon, but actually when full-blown is inclined to be creamy buff. It is best when very wide open, and should therefore be arranged a day beforehand if wanted for a special occasion.

Magnolia Fraserii has yellowish buff-coloured flowers. The shallow cups show a mass of dull-red stamens at the centre. Like all magnolias, they have an air about them, and this variety may be used in many ways. A well-shaped spray of it might be put in a shell such as is used in the picture on page 152.

During the winter we get various forms of eucalyptus which come over in quantity from France. Perhaps the best known is the variety called *globulus*; this comes in bud, but after the branches have been in water for a time the bud, most decorative in itself, sheds its pointed grey top and gives place to a beautiful cream-coloured flower, not unlike the flower of myrtle in general appearance. Another variety has little pointed buds that might have been cut out of ivory. These also open, and one has masses of creamy flowers on the branches. Eucalyptus is a really precious addition to a winter decoration. In leaf, in bud, in flower, it is beautiful at any stage, and it lasts for many days in water.

The flowers of hoya are of a most unusual colour. This greenhouse climber has heads of small star-shaped flowers which are really pale buff—very difficult to describe and very subtle in colour. As with lapageria one only cuts the heads, but these are useful for small vases—for the 'intimate' arrangements spoken of elsewhere. One head of this flower in a special vase is worth having for its intrinsic beauty, unusual colour, and sweet scent.

Perhaps the best small cream, or cream and brown, decoration can be achieved by making a mixed group. For this one has a variety of subjects. As well as tulip, hyacinth, Gloire de Dijon roses, one may have *Phlox Drummondii*, clarkia, stocks, and spireas. Zinnias may be had not only in deep cream but one sometimes finds a metallic brown among them. There are brown nasturtiums, brown toadstools, certain fruits and berries which may be used to act as foils for the paler-coloured flowers, and there is a rush, like a miniature bulrush, called *Typha angustifolia*, which is very pretty and one of the best of many good rushes.

The illustration on page 142 is of a bare branch which has what I call a corky stem; it is from an ornamental red maple. Set against a light background one gets beauty of line and shadow. It is worth taking pains to find a branch of really satisfying shape and it may be necessary to cut off a few twigs which spoil the general outline. Such a branch will last indefinitely—it may be used through a winter and put away for the summer and brought out again for use the following year.

It is fairly generally known that beech leaves may be preserved throughout the winter if they are placed, immediately after being picked, in a mixture of glycerine and water—seventy-five per cent of glycerine is a safe percentage, though I have used a fifty-per-cent solution for large quantities with fair success. The leaves should be picked before they have turned, or they may fall off the branches. Green beech leaves become somewhat coppery in colour, though much depends on the stage of development of the leaves.

The following list gives the names of yellow and cream flowers which are not discussed in this chapter or in the one on weddings, but which would be useful for decorative purposes.

Bulbs, Corms, and Tubers

Crown Imperial (*Fritillaria imperialis*). This is a most stately and interesting flower which was at one time to be seen in many a cottage garden. It is gradually becoming scarce, which is a great pity. The drooping yellow bells on a three-inch stem are surmounted by a crown of green leaves; the whole growth and character of the flowers is well defined, and there is no other quite like it.

Liliums

At present the various Backhouse hybrids are not very plentiful, but they are becoming less costly and may be grown from seed. Most of them are in shades of yellow, buff, and orange, spotted with brown or purple. They carry a number of reflexed flowers on tall stems, and are most desirable flowers.

Lilium umbellatum. There are many shades of orange and gold in this group of lilies. Golden Fleece is one of the best; it is golden yellow touched with scarlet at the tips, growing about two and a half feet high.

Lilium Willmottiae is a graceful lily bearing a number of small recurved flowers on stems covered with slender foliage. It grows easily and is inexpensive.

Tulips

If I could choose only two yellow tulips, I would have Moonlight and *retroflexa*. Both have slim, pale-yellow flowers borne on long, slender stems. The first has particularly long oval flowers of a delicate colour, and the second has beautiful reflexed petals.

The parrot tulip is most decorative and strange; although the heads seem too big for the stems and hang rather heavily, they arrange themselves in good curves; they are most valuable for mixed groups.

Annuals and Biennials

Poppies. There is a large double annual poppy of pale creamy yellow which grows two feet high, and which is unusually good. Messrs. Ryder sell the seed; they call it a Malmaison poppy (creamy yellow). It is one of the best and most useful of cream-coloured annuals.

Salpiglossis. There are several flowers in this group which have yellow and cream and brown colourings, and one can best pick them out from a seedsman's list. Yellow, brown and gold, and white and gold are all listed, and the richness of their velvet trumpets is of great value.

Sweet sultan, stocks, and verbenas may be had in yellow colourings, and the modern zinnias are magnificent in every shade of pale cream to deep metallic bronze. They are, I think, the most important annual in this colour for decorative work.

Perennials

Digitalis, or Foxglove. These flowers may be had in cream and pale yellow, and the tall spires of bells are full of character. Although really perennial, it is best to sow seed in late spring each year for blooming the following year.

Hemerocallis (day-lilies). These are sweet-scented, lily-like flowers, and although each fully-opened flower only lasts for a day, the buds open in water. There are several distinct good varieties.

H. aurantiaca major is deep orange with large flowers, and grows two feet six inches high. *Dumortieri* is yellow outside and orange inside, two feet. *Flava* is a clear yellow with a very sweet smell, two feet six inches, and *Middendorffii* deep orange-yellow, one foot six inches.

Papaver orientale. There are several oriental poppies sufficiently salmon in colour to be included in this list. Mrs. Perry (salmon pink), Princess Ena (salmon apricot), Orange King (deep orange) are a few varieties, and there are many more to be selected from the nurserymen's lists.

Primulas. Primula *helodoxa* carries whorls of yellow flowers on strong stems, excellent for cutting, and *P. sikkimensis* (Himalayan cowslip) is most beautiful with drooping pale-yellow clusters of sweet-scented flowers.

Shrubs

The azaleas make the most prolific contribution to flowering shrubs of the colours under discussion. *Azalea pontica*, the old sweet-smelling yellow variety, is one of the best for cutting. It grows freely, and one may cut long, delicate branches. The *mollis* varieties give us flowers in shades of flame and orange and rosy yellow.

There is a rare and beautiful yellow tree-peony which came to us from China. I am told it is not difficult to grow, but it is not very often seen in gardens.

Euonymus. An evergreen variety with white fruit-capsules and orange berries is exceedingly good. It is called *Euonymus radicans Carrierii*.

The berberises and brooms, forsythia and winter jasmine, *Rosa Hugonis* and the orange *Buddleia globosa* are all valuable contributions to yellow and orange flowers.

Greenhouse Flowers

Among the exotic-looking cannas there are some good yellows and golds, and these flowers are so spectacular that they are especially valuable.

Streptosolon is a free-blooming climber with orange flowers borne in clusters. It does not carry well, but if picked and put straight into water it lasts for two or three days.

Lachenalias bloom in the spring, and have flower-spikes of nine to twelve inches high. They are in shades of yellow, gold, and coral; some have greenish shading. They have spotted leaves, and one or two varieties may be had in bloom by Christmas. The flowers are both curious and beautiful. They are sometimes called Cape cowslips.

Celosias are annuals, and may be had in golden and scarlet. The flowers are like plumes, and are most effective in shape, while the colour of some varieties is almost startling in its intensity.

CHAPTER VIII

BLUE FLOWERS

I WAS once admiring the intense blue of a mass of anchusa in brilliant sunshine, and fell to discussing a blue flower-border with my host. I remember advocating some particular variety of delphinium, the name of which I have long since forgotten, but which was not pure blue in colour; and he leapt at me at once with: 'I like my blues plain, not mixed with mauve.' Well, so do I: but that is a very difficult standard to maintain throughout the year, and although this chapter is headed 'Blue Flowers' I intend to discuss blue, mauve, and purple flowers indiscriminately. The intense, deep blue that one gets in gentian, in *Salvia patens* or in anchusa; the clear pale blue of plumbago or hydrangea and of flax (*Linum perenne*) is by no means a common colour in flowers; and there are times of the year when 'plain blue' flowers are difficult to find. Nor does the difficulty end when you have found them, for blue flowers are by no means easy to use well indoors, and a mass of blue, satisfying in brilliant sunshine or against a foil of other flowers, may prove disappointing in different surroundings.

In the first place deep-blue and purple flowers do not light up well, and the paler colours may take on a greyish tinge when seen by artificial light. This is not always the case, and one must take into consideration the form of lighting available. Some modern methods of lighting do not have this effect. But whatever form of artificial light may be in use, blue and mauve flowers are seldom suitable for rooms decorated in dark or subdued colours; they look their best in white and cream rooms, pale-green or grey or primrose-yellow rooms. A bowl of gentians in a white room, blue water-lilies on a pale-green table, purple poppies against pale-yellow brocade, all conjure up pleasant pictures; but put your gentian against dark oak panelling, your blue lilies on a mahogany table, your poppies in a brown room, and all the thrill is gone. If, on the other hand, you have a dull silver screen, or some silver hanging, and try the effect of a mixed blue group against it, you will find that you can get many beautiful effects.

I suppose the most popular of all blue flowers is the delphinium in all its shades of blue and mauve. It is a fine flower and looks well alone or forming part of a mixed group. I used it lately with heavily-fruited branches of damson. The bloom on the fruits gave them a very blue tone which the delphiniums emphasized. A great many of the leaves were removed from the fruit branches, and the whole arrangement was pulled together by the use of a large flower of artichoke, and the result had a certain richness which the delphiniums alone would not have given, especially as the flowers were necessarily the smaller blooms that one gets in late August.

Another blue flower which might have been used for the same purpose is *Catananche caerulea* (Cupid's dart), but these would have been needed in profusion, and as they shut up at night the effect might have been spoiled.

Purple poppies would have been good in a different way. They would have detracted from the blue bloom of the damsons and turned the whole into a more purple group: but their great double heads would have looked very handsome. Shown on page 127 there is an arrangement of vines and damsons with white roses and purple border-carnations arranged in a small marble *tazza* about ten inches high. The grapes were grown in the open, and were tight bunches of very small berries. These, and the damsons, and the dull mauve carnations needed the white roses to lighten the group, and the whole arrangement, though small, was suited to the character of the vase, and the group was big in feeling. This is an example of a small-flower arrangement which might suitably find a place in a large room.

There are various berries and fruits besides the damson and outdoor grape of blue or purplish colour which are useful adjuncts to a blue flower group: certain of the berberis family, including the common form (*aquifolia*), the wild sloe, and the fruit of a plant called *Phytolacca decandra*; this last bears long racemes of close-packed purple berries which are most effective. There are two shrubs which I should like to mention for those who are interested in unusual plants. The first is *Decaisnea Fargesii*, which bears fruits which look like a purple broad bean—and the second is *Sino-franchettia chinensis* which bears long slim bunches of amethyst-like fruits. These are very beautiful and unusual. I got these shrubs from Aldenham House, and they appear to be perfectly hardy, although apparently somewhat rare.

We were once asked to decorate a suite of rooms entirely in blue flowers for some weeks in late May and early June, with a special request that the decorations should be unusual. My mind immediately leapt to all manner of things which would have been both unusual and exciting, but did not so readily register the limitations imposed by season and climate and by the lasting quality of the flowers I wanted. It was not for some time that I came to earth from a dream of ipomea and blue water-lily, gentian and blue polyanthus, passion flower and *Plumbago capensis*, and faced the simple facts that it was nearly June, that we were in the middle of a drought and a heat wave, and that the rooms to be decorated would probably be both crowded and hot. My lovely ipomea—the blue convolvulus of the old flower paintings—would not have lasted an hour, and the plumbago not much longer. There were no gentians, no passion flowers, and no polyanthus; but we did manage to get a few blue water-lilies which lasted for a day, and were well worth securing, even for so short a time.[1]

For the rest we used pale- and deep-blue clematis, agapanthus, and *Meconopsis Baileyi* arranged by themselves, and mixed groups of these and other blue flowers, such as love-in-a-mist, cornflowers, veronica, and phlox. Agapanthus gives to a blue group what an amaryllis does to a pink or red one—not quite so striking and solid, perhaps, but a great help. A really good head of deep-blue agapanthus is a beautiful thing.

Meconopsis Baileyi, the blue Thibetan poppy, is still almost a fairy-tale

[1] In a small pond in Mr. Norman Wilkinson's garden at Chiswick a small variety of blue water-lily used to do well all the summer, although the plants needed the protection of a greenhouse during the winter.

flower, with its silky-blue crinkled petals which open to reveal the mass of fine yellow anthers. A stem of it, covered with the lovely flowers and surmounted by the glaucous-green prickly buds, is full of character. It needs to be treated as other poppies, picked in bud and the tips of the stems dipped in boiling water. The buds go on opening when picked, and it lasts for several days. It may be arranged alone or used to give character to a mixed group.

There are many good clematises in varying shades of blue and mauve and purple, and they are of great value for their definition of shape and colour. They might have been used effectively instead of roses in the group illustrated on page 127, and in the shell shown on page 124. Both the buds and the full-blown flowers are most useful for table decoration.

Phlox Laphamii is a delightful plant about eighteen inches high, with large trusses of blue flowers of good colour, and it blooms in May and June.

For really handsome blue and mauve flowers we may turn to the allium tribe. There seems only one reason possible why these flowers are not more commonly grown, and that is because they belong to the onion family, and when the stems are cut or knocked, this is immediately obvious: but as with flowers of the ordinary onion this disadvantage lasts only while the flowers are being arranged and the stems out of water.

One of the finest of these is *albopilosum*; the flowers, which are star-shaped and deep lilac in colour, are borne in large heads on two-foot stems. They last when cut for many days. *Azureum* is about eighteen inches to two feet high, with intense blue flowers; *giganteum* is more rare than the two former: it is four feet in height, and has globe-shaped heads of lilac flowers.

But as well as the giants of the tribe, there are some smaller treasures— the variety *karataviense* grows only six to eight inches high, but it has broad grey-green leaves and large globular heads, borne in June, of deep-lilac flowers. *Beesianum* also grows about eight inches high, and has sky-blue flowers in July and August.

The taller varieties are handsome rather than pretty, and are valuable for obtaining bold and unusual effects. The white basket shown with gourds on page 133 never looks better than when it is filled with blue spring flowers; arranged thickly with gentians set in moss it is especially striking, and in turn we fill it with chionodoxas, scillas, muscari, and blue primroses. If these small blue flowers are arranged solidly enough, they are suitable for use in a big room. It is the broad effect of colour that one needs from them in these circumstances—the vase need not be particularly large, this basket is only about ten inches in diameter—but the blueness of the flowers should be emphasized by a solidity of arrangement and a sparseness of green leaves.

I think on the whole that one gets the best blue effects by using mixed flowers; in any case, I think if one had to produce a good blue decoration at short notice and without any special materials, one would do well to choose a mixed blue group.

In addition to the flowers and fruits already mentioned, the following list contains the names of a few flowers which it would be well to have, although of course these do not represent a tithe of what might be available.

Bulbs, Corms, and Tubers

Fritillaria meleagris, the snakeshead fritillary, has drooping elegant little bells which are patterned with dull purple or wine colour. They are valuable for their shapeliness and for the unusual effect given by the chequered colouring. This, however, is rather dull and subdued.

Helleborus orientalis, the lenten rose, may be had in shades of dull purple. They come at a time when flowers are scarce, and they have the same lovely shape as the Christmas rose. Before being arranged in vases they must be well soaked, and if they show signs of wilting, as they frequently do, they should be plunged in water, heads as well; they usually recover, and when once established in water will last for a long time.

Iris reticulata. I shall never forget the first time I grew a frame full of these flowers; I had read somewhere a suggestion that a violet frame might be devoted to them, and I tried the experiment. Their colouring of purple and gold, their scent of violets, seemed of peculiar richness and beauty on a cold February day. They are hardy enough to grow freely out of doors, but a frame saves them from being broken by rough weather, and for cutting this is the best way to grow them. Another winter treasure—and, to me, a never-failing source of amazement—is *Iris stylosa* or *unguicularis*. Any time from November till March you may find among the rather rough, strong leaves, pale-lavender, exquisitely delicate flowers. They should be cut in bud, when they carry fairly well, and will open their flowers, reminiscent of the conventional fleur-de-lis, and last for a day or two in water.

Muscari plumosum, or ostrich-plume hyacinth, is curious and attractive. The spidery, feathery flowers are a deep amethyst colour. They last for a long time in water.

Tulips

Among the May-flowering or cottage tulips there are certain varieties with stripes and variegations which resemble the tulips of old flower paintings. One of the loveliest of these is Dainty Maid, which has mauve markings on a white ground. Insulinde has purple markings on a pale-yellow ground. Some of the Rembrandt tulips also are striped and flamed with purple, such as Antique (white and purple), Eros (lilac and white with purple blotches), and Carolus Durand (purple and violet and white).

Annuals and Biennials

Arctotis grandis. This flower is one of the most valuable of annuals for cutting. The flower is like a delicate marguerite, with slender, pointed petals which are pale silvery-mauve on the outside and pearl-white on the inside. The centre is mauve, the stems and leaves grey. It grows about two feet high, flowers profusely and, if picked just before the flowers expand, lasts well.

Clary is good for its purple leaf-bracts at the top of the stems. It lasts for many days when cut.

Petunia. This is strictly a perennial, but is almost always treated as a half-hardy annual. The purple shades are very rich and strong, and of particular value in mixed posies, low bowls, or miniature 'Dutch' groups. There are several in the group shown on page 126.

Phlox Drummondii may be had in various shades of purple and violet, some with white eyes and some marbled in effect. They are excellent for cutting, but do not travel well.

Verbena. There is a rich purple variety called Violet Lady, and another called Hybrid Blue. The colour is very clean and good, and they grow readily from seed, so that they are usually treated as half-hardy annuals.

Perennials

Aquilegia. The long-spurred hybrids are very popular, but one rarely sees the lovely blue and white species called *glandulosa*, which grows about a foot to eighteen inches high, and is extremely beautiful.

Cobaea scandens is a climbing plant which bears reddish-purple bell-shaped flowers, rather dull in colouring, but worth having for their shape, which enables them to be used effectively.

Pentstemon. The purple florists' variety of this is excellent. The long spikes of bells, which vary from pale to deep mauve, last well and are most effective.

Polyanthus. Ryder's blue polyanthus is an excellent plant. It grows vigorously and bears numerous heads of flowers in varying tones of blue.

Salvia virgata nemorosa has long spikes of violet blue, and grows from three to four feet high. It lasts long in water.

Thalictrum dipterocarpum bears graceful purple flowers in profusion. The flowers are borne in large branching panicles, and the foliage is delicate and often described as looking like hardy maidenhair fern.

Shrubs and Climbers

Ceanothus. This shrub may be had in many varieties, and the blue flowers are beautiful and sweetly scented. Gloire de Versailles is perhaps the most popular. *Papillosus, Brilliant,* and *rigidus* are all good varieties.

Buddleia. The purple flowers of this shrub are valuable for cutting, and of the many varieties, *magnifica* with rose-purple flowers and *Veitchiana* with very long flowers, purple with an orange centre, are perhaps the two most generally useful.

Ceratostigmata Willmottiana bears flowers rather like plumbago in shape, and of intense blue. It likes the shelter of a wall, and when established, bears heads of bright blue flowers freely in the late summer.

Greenhouse Flowers

There are one or two greenhouse plants that were frequently represented in old flower pictures, and one still likes to use them in making groups. Fuchsias and pelargoniums were particularly popular. There are one or two of the former which are purple or mauve and white, and one may choose varieties from a nurseryman's list. Of pelargoniums there is one of deep velvety purple called Topsy. My plants came from Swanley, and are valued for cutting. The colour is most unusual, being of a rather blackish purple. Gloxinias are also valuable, but too fragile to carry. Their intense colours and velvety texture are always a source of delight, and they last for a day or two in water if cut before they are fully open, although it is a more common practice to use them growing in their pots.

CHAPTER IX

FLOWERS FOR WEDDINGS

In the opening chapters of this book I have expressed the opinion that flowers are not always allowed to take their rightful place in the general economy of a house, or in the preparation for a party; alleging that while food and clothes and general decoration are accorded specialized attention, the flower arrangements are left to take care of themselves. On the occasion of a wedding, however, this can seldom be said with truth; it is not unusual for a bride to plan her wedding so that the dresses match her favourite flowers, and as a general rule she selects flowers that will enhance the colour scheme of her bridesmaids' clothes. Certainly on this occasion the flowers come in for more consideration than the wedding-cake.

Whether the wedding be of the simple, pretty order, or partake of the nature of a pageant, the flowers play an important part. The bouquets should accent the colour scheme of the dresses, and the church flowers should form a beautiful setting without being so massive as to obscure the architectural features of the building.

Some people hold the view that a simple wedding is in greater accord with modesty and reverence, and therefore more in keeping with the solemnity of the occasion. Others consider that this is one of those rare occasions which may be suitably enriched with pageantry, that the wedding procession may be notable for its beauty, and the church *en gala*. They feel that all this may be achieved without marring the dignity and solemnity of the religious ritual. In either case there are certain guiding principles to be observed in planning a wedding. Primarily, it is well to remember that the bride and bridesmaids form a *cortège* which during the ceremony is seen as a whole; this calls for uniformity of treatment which does not end with the dresses of the bridesmaids all being alike. One is faced with the problem of a train of bridesmaids differing in face and figure, height and gait, each probably with views of her own as to how flowers should be carried, or wreaths worn, so that even when the bride has overcome the almost insuperable difficulty of choosing dresses and head-dresses that please every one, she cannot be sure that she has yet achieved her aim. Sometimes the bride herself will carry, for sentimental reasons, flowers which neither assist the general effect nor improve the appearance of her gown.

Orange blossom, the traditional bridal flower, is desirable from so many points of view that only the difficulty of getting it in quantity prevents it from being greatly used. It is deliciously scented, delicate in shape, and waxlike in texture—and romantic in its associations. In the time of our grandmothers it was used far more extensively than now; but in those spacious garden days most big gardens had an orangery, and great care and attention was devoted to the care and cultivation of orange trees, so that it was possible to obtain the small and precious blossoms in England. Nowadays there is little English orange blossom, and we rely on supplies from abroad, and I have been offered in the flower market a poor handful of rather bruised buds and flowers for a ridiculously large sum of money. Long ago, I remember seeing in a flower shop in Regent Street, long since gone from there, a large formal posy composed entirely of orange blossom, and its buds, surrounded by a frill of white paper and tied with white ribbons which had picoted edges—Victorian, delightful, and entirely romantic.

Perhaps the most popular bridal flower to-day is *Lilium longiflorum*. It is usually arranged in a sheaf and tied with ribbon or tulle. The sheaf is made long or short, according to the stature of the bride. Sometimes one is asked to add white heather or myrtle, or a spray of orange blossom for sentimental reasons. Small flowers added to a sheaf may destroy its dignity, and this can be avoided by fastening this small spray to the tulle or net with which the sheaf is tied.

A very formal arrangement of lilies may be made by attaching a number of flowers to one stem—the photograph on page 144 shows this. It is stiff and severe, but is suitable and effective with some wedding dresses. A similar arrangement may be made with arum lilies. The texture and colour of arums make them desirable as wedding flowers, and they are usually arranged in a sheaf. If this form of bouquet is not suitable, they may still be used in the form of a hand spray, as shown in the illustration on the next page, 145. It has definition without severity.

The hand spray illustrated on page 146 is made of white camellias. The flowers have been mounted on long wires which have been bound with gold gauze. The intention was to create an effect. This was carried with a gold dress, and the binding of the stems merged into this, so that the effect was star-like. The beauty of this arrangement depended entirely on its shapeliness and elegance.

The bouquet which is shown on page 147 would be particularly suitable for a white wedding, especially if the bridesmaids wore white tulle. The flowers are white camellias and they are surrounded by a frill of stiff white net which is edged with small silver spots.

Definition is a quality to aim at in flowers for public occasions—anything in the nature of a fussy bunch, even if it may look quite pretty at close quarters, loses even the quality of prettiness and becomes characterless and out of place.

Stephanotis makes a good hand spray, and with it one may use such foliage as myrtle or gardenia leaves—but not fern. The whole quality of stephanotis is lost when it is embedded in asparagus fern. Heads of lapageria, carefully mounted on wires, may be used alone or with stephanotis. The most beautiful bridal bouquet I have ever seen was of white magnolia—the variety called *conspicua* which flowers on bare branches. Three or four sprays only were used, but they were well flowered and perfect in shape. They were arranged in a long slim sheaf, and the line of the chalices and brown stems against the white wedding gown was strikingly lovely.

So far I have only mentioned white flowers, and I still think that an all-white wedding is the most beautiful; but often the bride carries

FLOWERS FOR WEDDINGS

white flowers while the bridesmaids have flowers to match or contrast with their dresses. I will therefore make a few suggestions of possible arrangements under colour headings.

Yellow, Flame, or Orange

Gerberas, with their lovely pointed petals, may be had in colours ranging from creamy white through yellow and pale flame to terra cotta. The paler ones may be mixed with yellow roses such as Roselandia or Golden Ophelia, the deeper one with the Talisman rose to get a stronger colour effect.

Yellow arums are dignified and beautiful, and may be used as sheaves or as hand sprays. They are best used alone and formally. Yellow freesias or orange tritonias are good in colour, but only available for a short period.

A mixed yellow or yellow and orange bouquet might contain a clivia, one or two yellow arums, a spray of yellow orchids, some gerberas and roses, and one or two other flowers of suitable colour. Azaleas, during their short season, are eminently desirable, although some kinds have to be treated with floral gum to make them last. From a colour point of view, they are invaluable, ranging as they do through every shade of cream, yellow, flame, and orange. If I knew someone with a Maréchal Niel rose-tree in bloom, that would be my own choice for yellow flowers. This rose is no longer seen in flower shops—nor is Niphetos, the lovely dead white 'bridal rose.' Their place has been taken by 'stiff-necked' varieties, and I suppose that from a practical point of view this is sensible. Perhaps my memory is blurred by sentiment because this was the 'party' rose of my childhood, but I do not think there is any other yellow rose so sweet or so delicate in colour as the old and much-loved Maréchal Niel.

Pinks and Reds

Bouvardia is another 'party' flower, and its rather salmon-pink colour is unusual. This delicate jasmine-like flower is best for small bouquets and for shoulder sprays. It is not an easy colour to find in flowers, though some of the gerberas match it in tone.

Lapageria rosea is good in colour, being a deep rose pink, and if it is obtainable in quantity, may be used for a hand spray. Even a few of its bells look well in a mixed bouquet with other flowers.

One of the prettiest pink bouquets may be made of camellias—rather formal, perhaps, but these flowers are so shapely and are to be had in so many good colours. Their own leaves are the only setting for them, although one must sacrifice a certain number of these or the bouquet would be too green. They look best arranged solidly in Victorian fashion, with a fringe of their own leaves.

For a pink sheaf there is one particularly desirable flower to be had sometimes in the autumn—this is pink nerine. It is a lovely glistening pink, and the long slender stems are suited for the making of a slim sheaf. These stems are good in themselves, and the flowers should be arranged so that some of them may be seen.

There are many flowers for making mixed pink bunches, and the following would help to give character to a mixture of the more ordinary kinds: pale pink anthurium, *Lilium Krameri*, Sirene tulip (though this delicate 'lily tulip' makes a good bouquet in itself), calanthes, belladonna lilies, and pink honeysuckle. We once did a very pretty wedding with geraniums in all shades of pink and red. These were massed into baskets for children to carry. Indeed this was the best way to use geraniums, for they would not have lasted if made into bouquets. We used many varieties, including some small-flowered scented geraniums, and the whole effect was unusual and good.

We were asked lately to make bouquets of different shades of red amaryllis, and were a little nervous that they might look too heavy; but with judicious arrangement and the elimination of a certain amount of thick stems they were most effective, and actually in the church the grandeur of the flowers seemed entirely suitable; they were as good red bouquets as I have seen.

Blues and Mauves

Blues and mauves present a difficulty; first because they do not light up well, and secondly because there are few flowers suitable for bouquets from which to choose. Delphiniums are frequently used, but I think I prefer agapanthus for a sheaf, and even this looks best mixed with some flowers such as pink lilies or pale anthurium.

The really exciting blue flowers, such as gentian, blue water-lily, *Salvia patens*, and plumbago, are difficult to manage ordinarily. They are lovely if they can be picked, arranged, and carried to the church all in an hour or so—but that premises a plentiful supply from the garden; so, though beautiful, these are not always practicable.

Sweet peas, scabious, and cornflower—of these I would choose the last, and have them arranged solidly with no fern or foliage.

Mixed flowers for bouquets are popular, and can be beautiful if the flowers are chosen with care. If they are too big or too coarse you may get a clumsy bunch, and this, carried by a preoccupied bridesmaid—as though she were holding a wet baby—will be a dire failure.

Baskets, once so popular, are difficult things to carry well; but for young children, whose natural grace and abandon enables them to look attractive in circumstances which make older and more self-conscious people look awkward, they may be used with discretion.

Bows are always a difficulty. Some bouquets must have them—others are better without; but it certainly is easier to carry a bouquet gracefully when it has a bow. Ribbon or tulle is usually chosen, but for some flowers one may take narrow lengths of organdie or fine muslin and have the edges picoted: these materials look particularly well with mixed bouquets.

Sometimes the use of a ribbon which actually matches a dress entirely destroys the value of a bouquet. In such cases a ribbon or tulle matching the green of the flowers may meet the case if one must have a bow at all.

Headdresses are very difficult: often a wreath that looks pretty in the hand may look ludicrous on the head. Flat leaves such as camellia or myrtle with flowers added at the most becoming spot are fairly safe.

Whole wreaths of myrtle leaves with their own flower buds, bouvardia, and jasmine, are all suitable, but when one tries to use larger and more solid flowers, great care is needed. I have seen solid, oval-shaped wreaths of gardenias and camellias look beautiful, but they were on small heads, very cleverly arranged, and were by no means suitable for every one.

The decoration of the church is the next consideration, and here one has to think not only of the individual wishes of bride and bridegroom, the setting of the *cortège*, and the proportions and feeling of the building, but the limitations and regulations imposed by those in authority. For so long it has been the custom to use palms and ferns and pot plants with very little variation, except in the magnitude and extensiveness of the decoration. The church authorities having for long years accepted this form of adornment are for the most part reluctant to let one embark on any decoration which they may regard as experimental. I think they fear that one may do some damage to the edifice—make extra work for the cleaners, or use flowers in a way not in keeping with the sanctity and dignity of the church—and of course it is possible that their fears might not be groundless; though in view of some Harvest Festival and other decorations seen, I cannot think there is much ground for apprehension provided the work is in the hands of a reasonably considerate and experienced person who will not willingly obscure any architectural or other beauty of the church.

On the whole I do not like what I call conservatory arrangements in churches. I prefer to use very large and beautiful vases and fill them rather grandly with cut flowers, placing these where they may be seen by the congregation and where they do not hide from view the bride and groom. These flower arrangements are usually placed about the chancel steps and at the altar rail, but details of this kind depend entirely on the arrangements in individual churches.

If one wishes to decorate the body of a church, there is one way which is both beautiful and traditional, and I can best give an idea of it by describing an actual wedding.

This wedding was in the country. The church was old, simple, and beautiful, and it was decorated in the following way: Four large vases of flowers such as I have just described flanked the steps leading to the chancel. Against twelve stone pillars, six on either side, were placed poles; these rested on the ground and stood out at an angle in the way one sees Venetian lanterns in old pictures. They had slings like sashes which passed round pole and pillar some feet from the ground. These poles were first bound with ribbon or muslin, and crowning each was a large bouquet of flowers tied with the same material that made the slings or sashes. At the centre of the aisle there was a similar arrangement. Two poles were placed one on each side of the aisle and secured to the end of a pew. In this case, however, the poles were upright and not standing out at an angle.

The vicar of the church thought this decoration beautiful and in keeping with the dignity of the building, and he had more reason than many to cherish its beauty. The effect was festive and gay, but not tawdry. It was traditional too, and in some way reminiscent of church festivals of early times.

There is a difficulty which nearly always arises when one comes to the decoration of the altar. One is generally required to use narrow-necked brass vases which have little beauty and which do not permit of any satisfactory arrangement of flowers. Sometimes one is allowed to use beautiful and suitable vases, but not very often. I wish I knew why. I can understand that one must not run any risk of vases that might fall over or leak because of the danger of spilling water on the altar cloth; but these brass vases are not always entirely safe. I wish I could have asked Dean Hole, for although he lived in most conventional times, I am sure he would have been sympathetic because of his love of all beautiful things, and his enormous knowledge of flowers: and I believe he would have told me what was the insuperable obstacle that almost always prevents one from making altar flowers look especially beautiful.

A wedding ceremony in a synagogue lends itself particularly well to good flower decoration. The bride and bridegroom stand under a canopy which is supported by four slender pillars. Beautiful materials are used for the roof of this canopy. I know one at least which is made of wonderful white brocade embroidered and encrusted with silver thread. The edges of this roof and the four pillars give one an opportunity to create good decorative effects. Garlands of flowers may be used and each pillar may be crowned with a slender plume of flowers—or the pillars may be built up into tapering columns of flowers.

I am often asked by young brides and bridegrooms to tell them what flowers are required for a wedding, and who usually bears the expense; and although the conventional ideas of former years no longer prevail, the general practice is as follows :

The bride's flowers are the gift of the bridegroom—although, nowadays she often chooses them herself, and decides on the price. The old idea of the gift of flowers coming as a delightful surprise on the wedding morning unfortunately is dead. The bridesmaids' flowers are also his gift, although if headdresses are chosen the bridesmaids sometimes pay for these themselves. In some cases the bride's mother, if she has very insistent views, will pay for their bouquets—this at any rate gives her a freer hand in having her wishes and tastes prevail.

Bouquets or shoulder sprays are usually ordered for the mothers of the bride and groom, and buttonholes for the groom and best man are generally white carnations or gardenias—and white or red carnations for the ushers. The payment for all these generally falls to the lot of the bridegroom.

The cost of the church decorations is usually born by the bride's family.

CHAPTER X

DECORATIONS FOR CHRISTMAS, FOR PARTIES, AND FOR RESTAURANTS

ALTHOUGH we shall doubtless return to them again, the once inevitable vases of holly and mistletoe, and ropes and wreaths of evergreen, are no longer the only acceptable forms of Christmas decoration. There is an inclination to seek variety of adornment for both house and table; even the popular Christmas tree has its rivals, but of that more later.

We certainly could not well do without evergreen and holly, but their use is modified. For instance, there is a pleasant fashion—foreign in origin—of hanging small wreaths in the windows of houses, setting lighted candles inside them, and leaving the blinds undrawn. Some people hang a wreath over the door knocker—it may be of holly or evergreen, and is sometimes frosted and bound with red or white ribbons.

Both these customs, if more generally adopted, would lend an air of festivity to the streets and would add to the pleasure of many people who love the excitement of Christmas but who are unable to afford such luxuries for themselves.

If holly is required for use on a table or for vases, it will be more effective if some of the leaves are removed from well-berried branches; in this way the bright colour of the berries is shown up, and the general effect is lighter than it would be if one used the whole of the foliage.

Last year we used a great deal of white and silver for Christmas. We cut shapely branches of different types and whitewashed them Some, such as larch branches, covered with small cones, were merely whitewashed or whitened and frosted; others were used to carry silver ornaments, tiny bells, silver balls, and glass and silver icicles. Some had the small white Cape flowers fastened to them, and all these were grouped together in large vases. They were gay and pretty. Of course this idea can be developed in any colour, but white seems most like Christmas.

Another pleasing decoration is a modern version of the old kissing bunch. I do not know where this idea comes from, or how old it is, but it was an inevitable part of Christmas when I was a child. It was made of three children's hoops placed inside one another, forming a globe; the hoops were decorated, and a bunch of mistletoe hung from the base. As children, we used frills of coloured tissue paper and gaudy ornaments to decorate the hoops, but now we cover the hoops with silver gauze or ribbon, the large bunch of mistletoe at the base is heavily frosted, and hanging inside this open globe is either a silver witch-ball or a silver bell. Half-way down each curve of the hoop are put glass icicles—one may add to this any silver or white adornment, but it is really most decorative if kept fairly simple. This is really lighter and gayer than a branch of mistletoe and serves the same indispensable purpose.

As children I think every year we expected the Christmas tree to look more like the story-book pictures of a Christmas tree than it ever did—and I think, aesthetically, we were right. The formality of the traditional tree is more pleasing to the eye than the unwieldy bushes of evergreen that are generally used. Not that I think for one moment we analysed this sudden and hardly registered disappointment when once the tree was decorated! Probably for children the ordinary green bush is best—it will carry heavy parcels, and if it were superseded too suddenly, there might be some disappointment, so the only thing is to use it; but it may be trimmed and pruned to improve its shape. It may also be slightly whitened and frosted in places. This makes it gayer, I think. The entirely formal and artificial 'tree,' which is illustrated on page 148, may please more sophisticated minds. It is made of three hoops—and in this case the hoops are covered with white paper roses and hung together with silver gauze. Sometimes the hoops are covered with whitened frosted holly—or one could use plain green holly or evergreen. The main point is formality. Tiny trees made in this way are good for the Christmas table. For a large table one might have three trees—a centre one larger than the others—and use silver candelabra between, or white flowers, or both.

The pieces of white holly to be found sometimes growing near the trunk of variegated holly-trees are very useful; they mix well with white flowers, or one may use them alone. Low bowls or shells filled with Roman hyacinths may be placed irregularly about the table; they do not interfere with the centre decoration, and add greatly to the general beauty.

One may use very tall candles standing in small wooden blocks (these may be bought for a few pence), and a wreath of flowers—rather wide and solid, made to surround the base of the candle. This again may be of holly leaves, green, or whitened and frosted, or of white or coloured flowers. Candles give height without interfering with the general conversation. If one possesses a suitable figurine or small statue, one may use this and surround it with a large flat wreath and then add small trees or candles.

Fortunately at Christmas one may really let the fancy roam and not be inhibited by fears of being too *outré*, too gay, or too ridiculous.

Parties

There is not a great deal to be said which applies exclusively to parties, except possibly this: it is best to keep party flowers high—really safely out of the way of guests—not only to avoid accidents, but so that they may be seen and enjoyed when the room is full of people. When arranging flowers for a party, visualize a crowded room, and you will probably be driven to the conclusion that the walls are the only places for flowers; and so they are. Mantelpieces, of course, if they are high, will do; but there is, after all, a limited number of mantelpieces in a room, and one may want a good many flowers.

And here we appreciate the utility of the wall-vase shown in the illustration on page 125. It is simple in shape and holds a large group—one such arrangement is enough to fill a considerable wall space, and it is extremely effective. The vase hangs on the wall at a suitable height, and the flowers are out of the way and may be seen and enjoyed. Sometimes a spotlight is arranged to shine on them, and this makes an excellent effect.

When one has to decorate a marquee for a dance one has to contend with walls which do not always carry the weight of a vase in the place one wants to hang it, and recourse may then be had to cheap baskets. These can be bent into such a shape that they may lie flat against the wall or be cut in half. One hostess last year suggested that we should use large rush hats hung by wide ribbons to the wall, and these were most effective. They were filled with masses of lilac and rhododendron in all shades of mauve and pink, both stripped of leaves, and peonies and other garden flowers. They were tied with apple-green ribbons and seemed entirely suitable for a débutante dance.

Swags of flowers on the walls, if well arranged, can form a dignified and elegant party decoration. The ropes of flowers should be solidly and evenly constructed, and be long enough to form graceful curves with ends to hang down between the curves. This takes an enormous quantity of flowers. One can, however, get an excellent effect by making these ropes of muslin or tarlatan and tying knots of flowers at intervals. If even this makes too severe a demand on the flower supply, try making the ropes of white tarlatan and tying formally arranged knots of evergreen at intervals.

One is sometimes asked to fill a fire-place with growing plants and ferns, or cut flowers and leaves. For a private house I am usually averse from this practice. The flowers look out of place, and the fire-place looks far better left in its normal state, especially if the grate is filled with the nicest logs that can be found. Silver-barked trees provide the best logs for this purpose. In a very large ball-room where banks of flowers are wanted one may build these up so that they completely hide the fire-place, but this is rather a different matter.

An amusing table decoration for a children's party is made of imitation cherry-trees with real cherries. We make these with small twigs and branches pruned into shape and wired together to form little trees; on these we fasten a few leaves and hang masses of cherries. They are really very pretty, and permission to eat the cherries is generally appreciated. This idea may be used in another way for a grown-up party; the trees are then adorned with camellia flowers and leaves. They last well, and if care is taken in the selection and pruning of the branches, they can have great elegance and beauty of line.

The foregoing remarks about party flowers really cover most of what I feel about restaurant flowers; but I think nothing short of an earthquake will bring about reformation here.

Even in the most expensive restaurants there is still to be seen that irritating little vase which is just in the way on the small table, and one either pushes it aside or an observant and obliging waiter removes it. Even if it is not a positive nuisance it is rarely an actual pleasure. Probably if you asked why these measly little vases were used, you would be told it was because there were so many tables that it would be too costly to do a really good decoration for each. But why do one for each? Why have flowers on the tables at all? Why not concentrate the supplies into one or two fine groups placed at vantage points? One would want high steady stands of good capacity, and these could be had in wrought iron or carved wood, or they could be made in mirrored glass. These in themselves would give scope for good effect and might be cleverly lighted. When filled with fine groups of flowers they would prove arresting.

It is part of the organization of most restaurants to send buyers to Covent Garden market to buy vegetables and fruit, and naturally, advantage is taken of this to obtain flowers from the wholesale merchants, but while the former commodities are entrusted only to experts, the flowers, not being regarded as an important part of a feast, usually fall into unskilled hands.

I wonder if one enlightened and progressive restaurant director were to set out to have his flowers so arranged that they were really exciting and beautiful—a matter of exclamation and delight—whether he would find that he had indulged his aesthetic sense at the expense of his business acumen, or whether people of taste and discernment would flock to his restaurant and reward him for his originality and courage. It might be tried perhaps in some of the special rooms set aside for parties in the big

London hotels, but here again there would be a stumbling block. Some of these rooms are magnificently decorated as to the walls, ceilings, and floors—lighted with consideration and thought for the appearance and comfort of the guests—but the tables lag behind. The same old damask cloths, the same ugly table-napkins—and one's eye comes back from the perhaps beautiful, but at any rate considered room, to the anti-climax of a perfectly ordinary, uninteresting table which is the centre of the feast—the cynosure of all eyes—and it is *dull, dull, dull*.

These tables could be greatly improved without unduly large expenditure. There are delicate-looking cloths and table-napkins which, if reasonably treated, wear as well as most damasks, and probably cost less to begin with, which would look less ordinary and more in keeping with these rooms, and would add to the general air of pleasure and festivity. Granted a fairly free hand, and a reasonable taste and discretion, a pleasant change might be wrought without any undue strain on the exchequer. If it were considered desirable to have flowers on these tables, they could be treated more individually than would be possible in the general restaurant, where some measure of uniformity is desirable.

I wish someone would try, even in a small and limited way, provided it was done with enthusiasm and intent to succeed, to see, in plain and common terms, if it would pay!

It has only recently become at all usual to see flowers in shop windows and showrooms; where they are done well and given due consideration they fulfil more than one purpose. They may be used to emphasize the general decoration, to give life to dull and otherwise uninteresting surroundings, or they may serve to draw attention to a display which has otherwise no particularly arresting power.

Where they are used in beautiful surroundings and in combination with other lovely things, the task of the person who undertakes to arrange them is a pleasant one. In such cases one has to enhance existing beauty, or perhaps to bring to life something which, though beautiful, lacks vividness. Given reasonable facilities for obtaining materials and a few happy ideas, one may find many ways of doing this.

In such cases the flowers need to be used with discretion, and will probably play an entirely subsidiary part: in a window, for instance, it will probably be unwise to allow them to overpower the rest of the window display, although they may be used to create the strongest note of colour—be, in fact, the high light of the whole scheme.

In a room used for the display of furniture or decoration they are best used to stress the colour or shape of some characteristic of the room, or to draw attention to similar qualities in a piece of furniture. Examples of this would be in the use of a red group on a piece of red lacquer furniture, or a dome of flowers, like the roses on page 123, in a niche; or the vase of grapes on page 151 against dim green brocade curtains.

The task, however, becomes more difficult when the flowers are needed to redeem a room or a display from dullness or even actual ugliness. It may then be a good plan to allow the flowers to overwhelm their surroundings. This may be useful where one wishes to attract the attention of passers-by to a shop window which has no intrinsic attractiveness, and where the objects to be displayed are not beautiful. This power of attraction in flowers is a very remarkable one. One may have a room full of beautiful things or a street full of shops all showing bright colours and desirable objects, and yet if one adds to all this one really good group of flowers it becomes a focus of attraction. The colours may be no brighter than the dresses and not as bright as the jewels, but the flowers are alive.

And by the very reason of their being living things, they may add attraction when properly used, or they may add dreariness to dreariness if not so used. It would be better not to follow the prevailing trend in this matter if for want of enthusiasm and interest the result is a vase of flowers ill-selected and carelessly arranged.

CHAPTER XI

VASES

I AM at a loss to know how to attack the subject of vases. There are so many things to say about them but no royal road, as it were, to be specific. Moreover, being a carping self-critic, I find a reason for not saying half the things I think—answering accusations about expense, unsuitability, risks, and general impracticability. I may as well admit about vases generally that a great many which I see filled with flowers I would rather not use for this purpose, and a great many that I see left empty I would like to use. So on this general note of contrariness I will open a very difficult chapter; and if it partakes too much of an expression of my personal idiosyncrasies rather than of an impersonal survey of the subject, perhaps this introduction will serve as an admission.

I rarely, if ever, set out to buy a vase; that is to say, an ordinarily recognized flower-vase, certainly never for my own use. But the antique-shops, the sale-rooms, and the junk-shops are constant sources of temptation to which I frequently yield, and my stock of vases is probably out of proportion to the other household equipment. This does not mean that I have spent large sums of money on vases, indeed the reverse is the case. Of course, if one finds a really fine vase of classic shape and proportions in an antique-shop, one may pay a considerable sum for it; and if it is possible to acquire it by dint of forgoing some other luxury (or I would even say necessity) one rarely regrets the effort. An exquisite vase is a perpetual inspiration, and, whether empty or filled with flowers, a pleasure and rest for the eye. An example of a vase which is a never-ending source of delight to me is seen in the illustration on page 149.

This vase is beautiful to look at whether empty or filled with flowers.

It is so heavy that it is not disturbed by the heaviest branches of fruit or blossom, and its soft, pale-brown colour enhances whatever one chooses to put in it. It is shown filled with a formal arrangement of arums which had a severe beauty, fitting it for a place where a lighter arrangement would have been unsuitable.

A vase such as this is not within the reach of all; there is, however, great satisfaction and interest for those of us with limited, even very limited means, in finding good shapes and sizes in objects which may need adapting and treating to render them suitable for the purpose in mind. An example of this may be seen in the illustration on page 129. This vase is of white alabaster, excellent in shape and colour, but as it is part of a big and very ornate vase, it has no base. The flowers are held in a tin lining which costs a few pence. There are a great many vases which may be so used. The too ornate Victorian examples may be looked at with this in mind: the chalice holding red roses on page 123, is part of such a vase. I sometimes see and buy old metal lamp containers—they are often of excellent shape but of poor metal and rough ornament. These, painted white, make good and inexpensive vases, and they are sometimes quite fit to take their place in a beautiful room. Stone or lead vases, such as the one shown on page 150, are delightful to use—they are so heavy and of a good colour. One can sometimes find old garden vases not too big for indoor use.

The vases in the illustrations on pages 126, 127, 132, 140, are examples of vases which needed no adaptation or alteration, but which were bought at a very small cost from time to time.

The small white vase shown on page 151 stands on a black marble plinth, the whole being about seven or eight inches in height. It is dignified, heavy in weight, will easily carry a miniature mixed group, or it may be heaped up with a mass of camellias and look important and rather grand.

Another example of small grandeur is the illustration on page 127. This a marble *tazza* about nine or ten inches in height. It will carry small branches of fruit or a tight flat posy of flowers—or may be heaped with small gourds. Filled with the heads of white roses it is a delight.

The cornucopia, shown on page 142, illustrates a type of vase that is rather sought after nowadays. A pair of these vases can look excellent in the right setting. One needs to arrange the flowers to emphasize the shape of the vase. Wall cornucopias are more easily found, and look delightful in small rooms, flanking a fire-place or a mirror.

Large shells may sometimes be filled and placed informally about a dining-table. The flowers should accentuate the curve of the shell and fall from it in a graceful way, fanwise, and may touch the table. There is a picture of a shell filled with nasturtiums on page 124 and another with tulips on page 152.

Nowadays one may buy delightful shells made of glass in white and blue and green. As they are modern, one may have as many as one can afford to buy.

The vase, on page 140, is a Devonshire pottery jar, whitened. These may be had in excellent shapes and all sizes: they are cheap and heavy enough to be safe and hold plenty of water. They are generally satisfactory, inexpensive vases.

The illustration, page 125, shows a modern vase of good shape made of papier mâché. It has a tin lining to hold water, and may be used hanging or standing against a wall. Its general utility is clear.

Vases to suit ultra-modern rooms are not always easy to find. There is a glass made for use in chemical laboratories which is often suitable for such rooms. It has a surface which looks like the extremely white and hard-frozen snow you may see on refrigerators in shop windows. This glass is made up into cylinders and tanks and bowls—good plain shapes and sizes—and although the dead whiteness does not suit all flowers, it does permit of arrangements which often exactly suit the requirements of a really modern room.

We are able to buy nowadays excellently designed, inexpensive, modern glass in every variety of shape and colour. This has almost superseded the ubiquitous cut-crystal of former days, and while its merits are obvious and one may look at it with admiration, I have a prejudice, perhaps stupid, in favour of buying what may be called odd bits and pieces. It seems to me that if one uses vases, or any other things for that matter, that are made in quantity, in every size and shape and colour, for the decoration of a house, one loses individuality and personality: but this is a personal idiosyncrasy, and there is no doubt that the modern glass is beautiful in design and admirably adapted to its purpose, and that one may find vases in plain, simple, elegant shapes in which flowers look well. I need hardly say that these remarks apply to inexpensive glass which is made in quantity, and not to the beautiful and, of course, costly individual pieces. One may possess or one may sometimes acquire at small cost those old-fashioned pieces of furniture known as *jardinière* tables. These are tables made with a zinc tray instead of an ordinary top, and were used for holding plants in pots. Small examples of these make admirable floor-vases to be filled with really large mixed-flower groups. The water and flowers are put straight into the zinc tray, and it is often an advantage to have a large and effective flower arrangement wherever you please without necessarily having to disturb the arrangement of the other furniture and ornaments in the room.

I am quite prepared to be laughed at about the vase illustrated on page 138. I once had a pair of them, and I know I shall hear them called rococo, ornate, and ridiculous; too curly, the winged animals too strange—in a word, monstrous—and the ridicule may all be perfectly just, but I like them. They are most amusing to look at and to arrange—they may be used in many ways, as they are in the photograph, filled with a pale 'dead' mixture, or filled solidly with lilies or with a great flat panache of arums, following the shape of the shell-shaped top. Or they may be heaped high with gourds. When I bought them they were covered with black paint, and looked really rather unpromising. There are to be found, from time to time, 'monstrosities' of this kind which need to be treated with paint or modified to enable them to hold flowers. They are splendid for a ball or for a party—or to stand on either side of a wide fire-place or flanking a console-table in a large room. I know they may not please every one, but I am not going to justify them any further.

If I may generalize a little, I should like to say that there are two ways of considering vases and flowers. One may either choose the flowers and then find a vase to suit them, or if you have a rare or lovely vase, make that your chief consideration and subordinate your flowers to your vase.

In any case, I would advocate that you do not put aristocratic and elegant flowers into 'peasant' vases—nor flowers with coarse stems or such as discolour the water into transparent vases. Nor do I think transparent vases are good for an arrangement with too many stems—one gets a confused effect.

One reads a good deal about the importance of proportion of flowers to vase, and though admittedly this is an important factor, I think it is good, sometimes, to treat the vase as entirely negligible, using it merely as a receptacle for water, and overpowering it if you will, so that the flowers absorb one's whole attention and the vase is unobserved. Indeed, if you wish to use your flowers, as suggested in the first chapter, as though you were using paints to get colour effect, you may have to do this.

One kind of vase I would never advocate, and I think I can say this without wishing to make any exception, and that is a vase which is painted or adorned with flowers in some way. If it is beautiful in itself it will, at best, be spoiled by the flowers, and in any case it will detract from the beauty of the flower arrangement.

Baskets, like bows, are difficult things, and in nine cases out of ten I would refrain from using them. There are a few good baskets and a few occasions when they are entirely suitable. Illustrating page 133 is a basket filled with gourds—it is an old one, round and shallow, with curved sides. I have tried to have it copied, but without much success, although the baskets which I have had made are quite pleasant in shape. This one is filled sometimes with gentians or other small spring flowers, sometimes with camellias. Delicate baskets of elegant shape are to be had quite cheaply, and are suitable for simple flowers, but never, never would I let a bow go near them.

The placing of vases when they are filled is not always an easy matter. Generally speaking, flowers look best with a solid background, and not with the light behind them. There are some exceptions to this—willow weed and bluebells, for instance, look best with the light shining through them—but an arrangement of flowers such as those in the illustrations on pages 128, 129, 130, and 149, would lose in quality and character if set against the light.

Sometimes one has a difficult background in the wall itself, and this may be overcome by the use of a hanging of such fabric as old brocade of suitable colour and unobtrusive design.

Reflections and shadows may add charm to the general effect, hence the peculiar value of a plain white wall or a highly polished table. In the illustration on page 122 is a little effect of shadow, but one can get this to a much greater degree in a dark table decorated with white flowers.

A mirror makes a lovely background for some flowers. Indeed, in some rooms it is the one place that one longs to be allowed to use for this purpose.

CHAPTER XII

AIDS TO FLOWER ARRANGEMENTS AND METHODS OF PRESERVING THEM — LONDON GARDENS

WITH every new flower-holder that comes upon the market new hope is aroused, but the flame only flickers for a moment. The perfect stand has yet to come. The best kind to be had, in my opinion, is still the solid glass block—its good points are that it is heavy and unobtrusive, and the holes which hold the flower stems are fairly big. Its foibles are that even the largest size topples over if you use very tall or heavy subjects, heavy stems break the thin glass between the holes, and the holes are graduated from a large one in the centre to quite small ones at the side, which is useless when you are using a number of flowers with big stems. Where the side branches are just as thick as the middle one, the glass block is inadequate. Wire netting rolled up loosely and fitted tightly into a vase is the best thing I know—and wire netting used in combination with a large glass block, if firmly wedged into place, will carry heavy arrangements of flowers in quite shallow bowls.

Sand is useful, especially when a vase needs to be weighted, and for dried flowers where no water is needed. For light flowers a few fronds of fern may be fixed in the vase to keep the stems in place.

None of these utilitarian accessories should be seen, and if any part of one is still in evidence after the last flower is in place, a leaf or two may be used to cover the defect.

Some flowers drink up a good deal of water, especially when first placed in a vase. It is therefore advisable to fill up vases to the brim and to look at them again some hours later. Neglect of this precaution is the cause of the death of many a vase of flowers. But I do not advocate as a general rule that vases should be emptied and refilled with fresh water each day. In the first place, flowers generally look at their best some hours after they have been arranged, and if you want your flowers for some particular occasion it is advisable to arrange them a day beforehand (though this, of course, does not apply to certain delicate and short-lived flowers), and the disturbance involved in changing the water would be detrimental to the general effect.

In the second place, the water in the vases has become of the same temperature as the room, and this seems to suit cut flowers; when you fill up the vases it is well to bear this in mind, and, in winter at any rate, one should use water with the chill off. I know it is a practice with some to take the flowers out of the vases, snip the stems, and replace in cold fresh water each day. I have not found this beneficial, and in some cases it would be actually harmful to the flowers themselves, which do not like to be handled, and certainly disturbing in the extreme to a carefully balanced group. Of course, if the flowers droop, something must be done. If roses or lilac or large chrysanthemums, or any woody-stemmed flowers, show a tendency to droop, one should take them right out of the vase, ascertain that the stems have been slit or peeled (or even hammered in the case of very tough stems), and then plunge them to their necks in a pail of warm water. For flowers very far gone one may use quite hot water. If this is done in time, the flowers will revive quickly, and probably not wilt again before their time. Most flowers last better if they are soaked for some hours before being arranged in vases, and certain subjects will not stand at all unless they have been first submerged in water. Some examples of these are arum leaves, maidenhair fern, *Bocconia cordata*, Bougainvillaea, and annual sunflowers. Observation and experiment will soon indicate a great many more cases when this treatment is beneficial.

Certain preservatives are sometimes advocated: aspirin, a tablet to a gallon, may be used for tulips and chrysanthemums, although if the flowers are soaked this is not usually necessary.

Hollyhocks, poinsettias, and poppies should have their stems either charred or dipped into boiling water for a few seconds before being soaked, and the last-named should be picked just as the buds are about to open.

Flowers picked for transport should always be soaked overnight; even if they travel by hand, and for a short distance, they will carry better if this is done.

The care and preservation of growing plants used for house decoration is a subject upon which many people seem either ignorant or careless. Plants are often bought during the winter because they last longer than cut flowers and are therefore deemed an economy; but there are many severe disappointments for those who do not know how to care for them. How often a fine azalea in full bloom is placed in a room and after a comparatively short time begins to show distress. It is often left alone, no doubt in a pious hope that it will 'come round,' until it is too late to be revived.

When plants have been cultivated for market-work they are kept in the smallest pots commensurate with successful flowering. The pots are full of roots, and in the cases of azaleas and heaths there is a tough fibrous ball of roots filling the whole pot and quite difficult to soak with water. If such plants are given small quantities of water at a time, the whole root may never get soaked. Indeed, if there happens to be a hole in the earth where a stake has been, the water may just run through this and not get to the roots at all.

The best way to water such plants and those which have to stand up to hot rooms and fires and artificial lights is to submerge the pots in a pail of water and leave them until bubbles of air cease to rise to the surface; and then allow them to drain; and this should be done as often as is necessary—in a hot room probably three or four times a week.

Plants dislike gas—some plants will not survive at all in a room with a gas-fire—even if the fire is not alight, if there is a small escape of gas they may drop their leaves and then succumb. They also dislike draughts, and will bear both heat and cold with greater equanimity than they will survive perpetual draught.

It is not within the scope of this book to discuss gardens, but perhaps a few comments about town gardens would be useful.

From a gardener's point of view, London gardens are an unsatisfactory and unsolved problem—one may take it generally that most plants will not grow well in the small, confined, overhung spaces allotted to them, though these spaces may be made gay and pleasant to look at. By growing, I mean literally growing from the first leaf into full flower, and the plants then remaining in a healthy state for the space of their normal life. Few plants do this well in London, and to have a satisfactory town garden one needs to put in plants each year which have been brought almost to their flowering stage in more congenial surroundings. This, of course, involves constant care and outlay.

The walls of town gardens could often be so much improved by changing the somewhat dreary, grimy background into a light and pleasant one by means of a coat of whitewash. This would need to be treated annually, but it is not expensive, and it helps enormously. Such a background gives full value to the branches and leaves of plants, so that even if growth is far from luxuriant, one may get a good effect from the curve and shape of some climbing plant whose thin branches looked nothing at all against a grimy brick wall.

Mr. Norman Wilkinson, whose taste and skill in all things appertaining to flowers and gardens was pre-eminent, first pointed out to me the value of vines and figs for London walls, and it was on his advice that I used Black Hamburg and Buckland Sweetwater grapes for this purpose. The shapely leaves are just what one wants in London, and their growth is such that one can clean the leaves and stems fairly readily. Moreover they often bear small branches of fruit which are most decorative. Small-leaved, thickly-growing plants get very dirty and unsightly, and are difficult to clean.

There is great winter beauty in the bare stems and branches of figs and vines, and this is a great asset in town.

Mixed hyacinths planted from boxes in the spring, and later *Lilium longiflorum* from pots, are effective and sweet-smelling, and last a reasonably long time. Mixed flowers are gay, but they need to be well-grown pot-plants and not seedlings when they are planted out.

Mr. Wilkinson has made one invaluable contribution to the problem of beautifying gardens in the flower-pots which he designed and caused to be made. One of them is shown containing the Christmas tree, on page 148, and this is only one of many good shapes. The large sizes filled with growing flowers make, I think, a far better effect in London than the usual small flower-beds: and one then has the opportunity for renewing the soil each year, and this gives plants, which otherwise drag out a weary existence, a chance to flourish even for a short season.

These pots are best whitewashed; in the spring Mr. Wilkinson used to fill his with double daisies (*Bellis perennis*) and polyanthus, and throughout the year kept them filled with a variety of plants which flourished exceedingly.

A very pretty effect may be made in an entirely shady border with moss, interspersed at intervals with small plants of all sorts. The moss must be taken up with plenty of earth, replanted at once, and watered well in; the ground should be watered before planting, and the moss soaked afterwards. It must be watered constantly all through the summer or it will turn brown and die, but it is well worth the pains. The small plants are unevenly scattered about the mossy bed, and the whole has a tapestry-like effect. If one has to buy the moss, this is a fairly costly matter, for one needs a large quantity to create any effect, since it has to be planted in a solid sheet covering the earth. It makes an admirable substitute for grass when the direct rays of the sun do not reach it.

The most important general factor in keeping a town garden sightly is cleanliness. Stone flags should be perpetually washed, pots whitewashed and leaves syringed. If care is taken in this way, the whole appearance of the garden may be pleasing, even though the number of plants is limited.

Since I finished this book we are all poorer by the loss of Sir William Lawrence and Mr. Norman Wilkinson.

Mr. Wilkinson's wealth of knowledge about both the growing and arrangement of flowers was always shared generously with those who knew him. His discrimination and taste in every form of decoration were an inspiration. I have had help and encouragement from him for many years, and I, together with many others, will miss him sadly.

The name of Sir William Lawrence is known the world over among gardeners and garden-lovers. It was he who first suggested that I should write a book about flower arrangements, and a few weeks before he died he wrote the foreword.

He was a famous and very much occupied man, but not too busy to seek out and encourage any one who showed interest in flowers. He came to see me some time ago because he had seen a flower arrangement of mine that had pleased him, and afterwards he used to come and see me from time to time and it was his approval which gave me the courage to try to express my ideas on paper.

APPENDIX

APPENDIX

ACHILLEA. A hardy border perennial.
A. Eupatorium or *filipendulina*. A fine form of yarrow. Three feet high. Flat yellow head of distinctive shape. May be gathered when fully out and hung in a cool shed to dry for winter use. If the heads are dipped in boracic powder the colour is preserved. There are many other varieties; perhaps the best known is *A. ptarmica*, The Pearl, bearing masses of small white flowers which last well in water. The variety *A. ptarmica*, Perry's White, has larger flowers. 28, 29.

ACORNS. 26.

AGAPANTHUS (African Lily). A bulbous plant, not entirely hardy, and therefore frequently grown in tubs and taken under cover for the winter. In mild districts it may thrive at the foot of a south wall if its roots are protected in winter. The blue variety, *A. umbellatus*, grows 2 or 3 ft. high and is splendid as a cut flower. 14, 22, 29, 35, 74, 85.
A. albus is the beautiful white variety. Large umbels of flowers on 3½-ft. stems. Agapanthus flowers in late summer and should be planted in early spring in rich turfy loam and be well watered and fed with liquid manure during the summer. 35.

AGROSTEMMA. Hardy perennials easily grown. *A. coronaria*, an old-fashioned border-plant with silvery-grey leaves and crimson flowers. *A. coronaria purpurea* is a very rich colour; it is best treated as a biennial. 54.

ALLIUM. Bulbous plants of easy cultivation. One or two suitable for naturalizing in woodland but for the most part liking sun. 27, 45.
A. albopilosum. A handsome variety bearing large heads of lilac flowers with grey foliage, height 2 ft., suitable for the flower-border. 75.
A. azureum. Blue. Flowers in July, about 18 in. in height. 75.
A. giganteum. A very handsome variety. Bright lilac in colour, growing 4 ft. high. 75.
A. karataviense. A low-growing variety about 6 in. in height with reddish-lilac globular flowers and broad grey-green leaves. 75.
A. neapolitanum. White starry flowers in May, suitable for naturalizing in woodland, 12 to 15 in. in height. There are many other varieties. 35.

ALYSSUM. This hardy perennial is usually grown in rockeries and makes fine masses of golden yellow in spring. The lemon variety called *citrinum* is a good colour. 28.

AMARYLLIS BELLADONNA. An autumn-flowering bulb of great beauty; the pink flowers are lily-like in shape with a delicious scent and are borne 5 or 6 heads in a cluster on stems 18 to 20 in. long, which are reddish in colour and covered with a delicate bloom. The flowers come up in September and October and the leaves follow in the new year. These plants need the shelter of a south wall, good drainage, and a light mulch of leaves in winter, and they dislike being disturbed. 26, 27, 43, 57, 60, 84.
A. Belladonna purpurea is a richer-coloured variety and has flowers of rich purplish-rose and a white centre and blooms earlier than other varieties. These flowers last for days in water but will only carry well if picked in bud, as their delicate petals break easily.

AMARYLLIS HIPPEASTRUM. Bulbous plants for the greenhouse. These fine lily-like flowers may be had in red, pink, and striped varieties. They are exceedingly handsome and it is worth while growing even a few plants. If there is accommodation which will allow of the pots being plunged in gentle but steady bottom heat the bulbs may be planted in December. If only ordinary greenhouse accommodation is available, February or March is a better time to pot them. These flowers last well in water, and cut in bud will travel well, open perfectly, and remain in good condition for several days.

ANCHUSA. Annuals and perennials. The best varieties of this plant are the perennials. 72.

A. italica. Deep blue, 5 ft. 29.

A. italica Dropmore. Brilliant blue, 5 ft.

A. italica Opal. Sky-blue, 5 ft.

A. italica Pride of Dover. Sky-blue, 5 ft.

A. myosotidiflora. Two feet. Like large pale-blue forget-me-not. Although perennials, old plants of these anchusas sometimes die after flowering, and it is a good plan to cut up the thick fleshy roots into 2-in. lengths and plant them in boxes of sandy soil in order to secure a reserve stock of plants.

ANEMONE, JAPANESE. 22, 27.

ANTHURIUM. Stove plants bearing brilliant flower-spathes. Red, pink, and white. Leaves also beautiful. 31, 43, 51, 60, 84.

AQUILEGIA. Hardy perennials. The long-spurred hybrids are the most popular. It is worth growing seed annually of these and treating them as biennials. Two good species are: *A. caerulea*, the Rocky Mountain columbine, which has pale-blue flowers with white centres blooming in June and July.

A. glandulosa. A rare kind, 12 in. in height, with large flowers, brilliant blue in colour; it is best suited to rock gardens. 78.

A. Stuartii resembles *glandulosa*, but is larger and more free-flowering.

ARBUTUS. Ornamental evergreen trees or shrubs. 49.

ARCTOTIS GRANDIS. Half-hardy annual. Flowers the shape of delicate marguerites. Outside of the petals greyish-blue and inside pearly-white. The centres are mauve and the stems and leaves grey. They grow about 2 ft. high and are valuable as cut flowers. The buds expand in water and the slender stem assumes graceful curves. Grown or arranged in association with grey foliage plants their delicacy of colouring and shape is accentuated. 50, 77.

ARTEMISIA. Hardy herbaceous plants which are valued in most cases for their fragrant or ornamental grey foliage. 46.

A. Abrotanum is best known perhaps as Lad's Love or Southernwood. A sweet-scented old-fashioned plant which may be dried for use in potpourri or for use among linen. 21, 50.

A. lactiflora. Sweet smelling, valuable for its creamy-white flowers, borne in plumes 4 to 6 ft. in height; a valuable border plant.

A. nutans is a graceful plant with pretty silver leaves. 50.

A. Stelleriana has foliage which is almost white. 50.

ARTICHOKE. Green. 45, 46, 73.

ARUM. The white and yellow arum lilies sometimes called callas, sometimes richardias, will be found under the latter name in this list. The best-known variety of true arum is the wild cuckoo-pint, the 'lords and ladies' whose curious green flowers or brilliant seed-heads may be found growing in hedgerows and in damp shady places in woodland. 23, 26, 28, 51, 53, 82.

A. Dracunculus is a most handsome plant. The flowers have large, deep wine-coloured spathes with an almost black spadix, mottled stems, and elegant leaves. The tubers should be planted in autumn in a half-shady border where there is plenty of moisture and shelter. 54.

A. palestinum is a handsome plant, purplish-black inside and green outside the spathe. It requires a warm and sheltered position. 34.

ASPARAGUS. Seed. 27.

ASPHODEL. Hardy perennial plants. The variety referred to in the text is *luteus*. The yellow flowers are not as decorative as the seed-pods, which are large, green shiny spheres. The size of a large black

APPENDIX

currant set thickly on the stems; have great character. 27, 45.

AUBRIETIA. Dwarf, hardy rock plants. 28.

AZALEA. 29, 71, 83.

BAY LEAVES. 33.

BEGONIA. Greenhouse plants valuable for both flowers and decorative leaves. 13, 15.

BELLIS PERENNIS. The double daisy is a most useful early spring flower. It blooms in a prolific manner and for a long time. It will bloom well in a town garden and in pots. When it has to be removed to make room for other flowers it should be divided and the flowers replanted in a piece of spare ground and not allowed to get too dry. The variety Rob Roy is deep red with frilled petals, and Dresden China has dainty pink flowers. 106.

BERBERIS. Evergreen or deciduous shrubs, valued for their brilliant foliage, berries, and flowers. 29, 71, 73.

BERGAMOT. See *Monarda didyma*.

BERRIES. 28, 32, 34, 65, 68, 73.

BLUEBELLS. 26.

BOCCONIA CORDATA or Plume Poppy. Herbaceous perennial, 8 or 10 ft. high, plumes of creamy flowers. The leaves are of glaucous green and greyish-white on the undersides. 65.

BOUGAINVILLAEA. Climbing plants usually grown in greenhouses. They may, however, be planted out in the summer months from pots. The flowers are inconspicuous but are surrounded by brilliant leaf bracts, the colour being a purplish-magenta. The variety Mrs. Butt has more red in its colouring than purple, and may be described as rosy-magenta. It is a fine form. 15, 27, 53, 54, 60.

BOUVARDIA. Greenhouse plants. Flowers resembling jasmine, in white and shades of salmon, pink, and red. 83, 86.

BROAD BEANS. 46.

BROOM. See Cytisus.

BUDDLEIA. Hardy shrubs. *Globosa* has flowers like small golden balls and blooms in August. Other varieties produce their flowers in racemes, mostly in shades of purple and lilac. 27, 29, 41, 71, 79.

CABBAGE. 15.

CACTUS. 22.

CALANTHE. An orchid of easy culture. Flowers white, mauve, and pink. Delicate and long-stemmed. 84.

CAMELLIA. A cool greenhouse shrub which may be grown out of doors in warm countries. 13, 14, 32, 46, 59, 82, 84, 93.

CAMPANULA. 29.

CANDYTUFT (*Iberis*). Annuals and perennials. 28.

Iberis sempervirens flowers in May, for dry walls, covering rocks or the front of a border.

I. gibraltarica, lilac-pink flowers.

Little Gem, masses of white flowers for rockery. The annual varieties may be had in rich colours of mauve, purple, and wine, and make fine bushy plants. They may be sown in autumn or spring where they are to bloom.

CANNA. Exotic-looking flowers for greenhouse or garden. The rhizomes need starting in a warm greenhouse and may be planted out in rich soil in May. The colours are shades of yellow, orange, salmon, and red, and some are spotted with purple and crimson. 58.

CARNATIONS. 12, 15, 28, 53, 54, 73.

CATANANCHE CAERULEA. Perennial plants with daisy-like flowers 2 ft. high, bearing many blue flowers on wiry stems. 73.

CEANOTHUS. Beautiful blue flowers, shrubs suitable for walls. 29, 79.

C. azureus, flowering in July, pale-blue flowers.

C. Gloire de Versailles. Blue flowers in summer and autumn. 22, 78.

C. rigidus, deep-purple flowers.

These are three good kinds.

CELOSIA. Half-hardy annuals suitable for bedding out or for pots. Sown in heat in April they may be planted out in June. The colours are scarlet, purple, and orange, and are very fine. 71.

CERATOSTIGMATA WILLMOTTIANA. A 4-ft.

shrub with bright-blue flowers like plumbago in late summer. 79.

CHAMAEROPS. 34.

CHINCHERINCHEE. See Ornithogalum.

CHIONODOXA (Glory of the Snow). Spring-flowering bulb. 21, 76.
C. alba. White.
C. grandiflora. Large lavender-blue flowers.
C. Luciliae. Brilliant blue with white centre.
C. sardensis. Gentian blue.

CHRYSANTHEMUM. 58, 103.
C. rayonnante is unique in shape with long spidery petals. One may have it in yellow, pink (a soft dull pink), white, and buff. The two last are particularly beautiful. This variety lasts a long time in water and is a valuable cut flower. 65.

CLARKIA. 39, 58, 68.

CLEMATIS. Shrubby and herbaceous climbers and plants. 29, 74, 75.
C. montana is a climbing species bearing quantities of white flowers in late spring. 42.
C. montana rubens has pale-rose flowers. 13, 59.
C. vitalba is the wild variety known as Traveller's Joy or Old Man's Beard. Of the large-flowered hybrid clematis there are many types, and care has to be taken in discriminating between these at pruning time as some bear flowers on old and some on new wood. Of the herbaceous kinds *C. recta* is an erect bush covered with small white flowers and *C. integrifolia* has small deep-blue flowers.

CLIVIA. Evergreen greenhouse plant, bearing in spring lily-like flowers in shades of yellow and orange. Good drainage and good soil are required, for the plants flourish undisturbed in their pots for many years. Quarter-inch bones and broken charcoal are a good compost. Water well from February to August, while plants are in full growth, then harden off and keep in cool, airy, frost-free quarters during the winter. When flowers are wanted return plants to closer quarters and give a little extra heat. 29, 83.

COBAEA SCANDENS. A tender climbing plant which may be grown in a greenhouse and planted out in late May or June. It is unlikely to survive the winter out of doors but may be flowered from seed sown in heat in early spring. The purple bells open in late summer. 78.

COLCHICUM (Meadow Saffron). Large crocus-like flowers in September and October. White, mauve, purple, rose, and wine-coloured. Single bulbs bear masses of flowers, foliage appears in spring. 35.

CORNFLOWER. 22, 28, 74, 85.

COTONEASTER. Valuable berried shrubs for winter decoration. 28.

CRAMBE CORDIFOLIA. Ornamental seakale, growing 6 ft. high like giant gypsophila. 40.

CRATAEGUS. A group of trees and shrubs bearing brilliant berries in autumn. 28.

CRINUM. Fine bulbous plants, flowering in late summer. They somewhat resemble the belladonna lily. *C. Powelli* is rose-coloured, and *C. Powelli album* white. They require shelter if grown out of doors. 36.

CROCUS. The spring crocus is so beloved that the only question concerning it is what colour to choose and how many can be afforded. The crocus species are less well known but exceedingly beautiful. 28.
Two good *autumn-flowering* species are:
Sativus. Purplish-lilac, feathered.
Speciosus. Violet-blue with darker veins, very fine.
WINTER-FLOWERING. The flowers should be protected or grown in pots in cold houses.
Chrysanthus. Gold and brown.
Imperati. Bluish-white and deep-purple veins, sweet-scented.
SPRING-FLOWERING.
Biflorus. White-striped purple.
Susianus. Golden yellow and brown.
Versicolor. White-striped and feathered with purple.

APPENDIX

CROWN IMPERIAL (*Fritillaria imperialis*). A fine old-fashioned plant 2½ ft. high with red, yellow, and orange blooms. Plant in autumn and leave undisturbed. 26, 69.

CURRANTS. White and red. 26, 34, 54.

CYCLAMEN. 12, 35.

CYDONIA. Shrubs for walls, bearing beautiful flowers and fruit. 42, 49.

CYTISUS (Broom). Hardy shrubs, flowering in late spring and summer. The white variety *albus* is the Spanish broom. 42, 71. *C. praecox* has primrose-yellow flowers, and *pallidus*, the moonlight broom, has lovely deep-cream flowers. Broom transplants badly and it is wise to plant it from pots into the garden.

DAFFODIL. 21.

DAHLIA. 15, 27, 53.

DAMSONS. 27, 29, 45, 73.

DAPHNE MEZEREUM. A shrub bearing pinkish-mauve flowers in February. The flowers are packed close round the stem and are exquisitely scented. It is one of the best early-flowering shrubs. It likes its roots in shade and its branches in the sun, and flourishes when protected by such light foliage as Japanese maple. There is a white variety. 59.

DATURA. A white-flowered, sweet-scented greenhouse shrub. 43.

DAY-LILY. 29, 66, 70.

DEADLY NIGHTSHADE. 28.

DECAISNEA FARGESII. Shrub bearing violet fruits. Requires shelter. 74.

DELPHINIUM. 27, 29, 45, 73, 85.
  D. Moorheimii. White delphinium. 40.

DIANTHUS. 13, 20, 28.

DIELYTRA SPECTABILIS (*Dicentra*). Pink racemes of flowers in May in the garden, or may be satisfactorily forced for the greenhouse. 58.

DIGITALIS. Foxgloves. Best treated as biennials. White, primrose, and spotted varieties are all worth growing. 31, 40, 70.

DIMORPHOTHECA AURANTIACA. An annual flower like a marguerite in all shades of cream, yellow, and orange. Good as a cut flower. 20.

DOCK. 46.

ELDER. 67.

EREMURUS. Stately herbaceous perennials which like shelter from winds and morning sunlight protection and deep loamy soil. 27, 58.
  E. Bungei. Golden yellow. July, 5 to 6 ft. 63.
  E. himalaicus. White. June, 6 to 8 ft. 36.
  E. himrob. Blush. June, 8 ft.

ERYNGIUM GIGANTEUM. 46, 65.

EUCALYPTUS. 46, 67.

EUONYMUS. 71.

EUPHORBIA WULFENII. Fine evergreen bush, 3 to 4 ft., large heads of greenish flowers. 27, 47, 66.

FERN. Maidenhair, 50.

FIG. 14, 105.

FLAX (*Linum perenne*). A slender, elegant, blue-flowered perennial, 15 in. in height, blooming in July and August.

FORSYTHIA. Spring-flowering shrubs bearing yellow bells on long leafless branches. 71.

FOXGLOVE. See Digitalis.

FRANCOA RAMOSA (Bridal Wreath). Cool greenhouse plant with long graceful spikes of white flowers. 12, 43.

FREESIA. 83.

FRITILLARIA MELEAGRIS. Bulbous plants with drooping elegant bells in April and May, usually in shades of dark purple and rose. 76.
  F. meleagris alba. White flowers. 36.

FRUIT. 17, 26, 28, 32, 45, 46, 64, 65, 68, 73.

FUCHSIA. 27, 79.

FUNKIA. 50.

GARDENIA. Greenhouse shrub. 13, 17, 32.

GARRYA ELLIPTICA. An evergreen shrub with long pale-green catkins in midwinter. 48.

GENTIAN. Some of the best dwarf kinds of this intensely blue flower are *acaulis*, *Farreri*, *verna*, and *sino-ornata*. 28, 74, 76.

GERANIUM. Herbaceous border perennial. 15, 22, 26, 27, 43, 50, 53, 54, 60, 61, 84.

GERANIUM, ZONAL.
Attar of Roses. A scented-leaf variety. 21.
GERBERA. *Gerbera Jamesonii hybrida*, or South African daisy, may be grown in south borders in warm districts but is more grown as a pot plant. The delicate marguerite-shaped flowers are in all colours from white to deep orange and red through all shades of flame and rose. 83.
GLADIOLUS TRISTIS. A June-flowering species of gladiolus with fragrant white flowers, 2½ ft. in height. Needs protection in winter if grown out of doors. 47.
GLOXINIA. Bulbous stove and warm greenhouse plants. 15, 32, 79.
GODETIA. 39, 58.
GOURDS. Ornamental, decorative, coloured fruits, grown in the same way as vegetable marrows; they do well trained up wire fencing. There are many varieties, white, green, green and white, striped, yellow, orange, in many shapes and markings. If picked when ripe they last for many months without shrivelling. 33, 49, 65.
GRAPES. 17, 28, 29.
GUELDER ROSE. See Viburnum.
GYPSOPHILA. Border perennial. Bristol Fairy is a good variety for drying for winter use. 40.
HELICHRYSUM BRACTEATUM. An annual flower growing 3 ft. in height in many colours of red, gold, orange, yellow, cream, and white. Valuable for winter decoration. They should be cut before they are quite open and be hung head down in a cool shed in their bunches to dry. 39, 40, 65.
HELLEBORE. *Helleborus niger*, the white Christmas rose, flowers from December to March. Flowers should be protected with hand lights. 17.
H. maximus flowers earlier and the outside of the petals are rose-tinted.
H. orientalis is the lenten rose, which ranges in colour from rose to purple to white. 76.
H. viridis has green flowers. 47.
HEMEROCALLIS. Day-lily. 29, 70.
HEMLOCK. 46, 64.
HEUCHERA. 40.
HOLLY. 46, 89.
HOLLYHOCK (*Althaea rosea*). A hardy perennial, best treated as a biennial. 40, 58, 103.
HONESTY (*Lunaria biennis*). Hardy biennial, useful mainly for seed-pods. There is a purple- and a white-flowered variety. 14, 40, 46, 65.
HONEYSUCKLE or *Lonicera*. 84.
HOPS. 65.
HOYA. 67.
HUMEA ELEGANS or Incense Plant. This extremely fragrant subject is a biennial. The seeds do not always germinate freely. A mixture of coarse brick rubble with the compost is helpful in this. It may be grown in pots in the greenhouse and planted out in summer. 66.
HYACINTH. 12, 68.
Hyacinthus (Galtonia) candicans. Bulbous plants bearing tall stems 3 to 5 ft. high of white bell-shaped flowers in summer. 36.
Hyacinths. Roman. 17, 91.
HYDRANGEA PANICULATA. 65.
IPOMEA (Morning Glory). Convolvulus-like climbing plants. *I. purpurea* is also known as *Convolvulus major*. 74.
I. rubro-caerulea has sky-blue flowers.
IRIS. 26, 29, 45.
I. pallida aurea. A variety grown for its variegated leaves. The flower is conspicuous. 50.
I. reticulata. A winter-flowering bulbous iris. Deep purple and yellow in colour, with a delicious scent. Perfectly hardy, but as it flowers in cold, rough weather, may be given cold-frame treatment in order to secure perfect blooms for cutting. 76, 77.
I. stylosa (unguicularis). A winter-flowering iris of great beauty and delicacy of colour and shape. Likes a dry situation at the foot of a greenhouse wall in gravelly soil. The flowers are surrounded by rough leaves and should be picked in bud. 77.
I. susiana. The Mourning Iris. Immense flowers finely veined with deep purple.

IRIS—*continued*
They flower in May and are about 18 in. high. *I. susiana* need a hot dry situation and protection in winter. The flowers are easily destroyed by rough weather and for cutting purposes may be grown in pots and brought into the greenhouse when the buds show. They must not be forced. 16, 27, 34.

I. tuberosa (The Snakeshead Iris). Soft green flowers with black falls in March, 9 in. high. Hardy, but may be slightly forced to bloom in February. 14, 46.

IVY. 14, 50.

IXIA. Bulbous plants bearing brilliant flowers on wiry stems 15 to 20 in. long. They are generally grown in pots but may be grown outside on raised beds if protected in winter. 26.

I. viridiflora. Sea-green flowers with black centres. 48.

JAPONICA or Japanese Quince. See Cydonia.

JASMINE. 13, 26, 86.

KALE. 15.

KALMIA. Evergreen shrubs. 59.

K. latifolia. 4 to 6 ft. high, bears exquisite pink flowers in June and July.

LABURNUM. 64.

L. Vossi. The hybrid *Vossi* bears long racemes of flowers and blooms later than the ordinary variety. It is a fine flower for cutting.

LACHENALIA. Small spring-flowering bulbs suitable for pot culture, 5 bulbs to a 6-inch pot. Many have green as the predominating colour with red or yellow tips to the slender bells. The stems are often spotted. 71.

LAD'S LOVE. See Artemisia.

LAPAGERIA. Greenhouse climber bearing drooping wax-like bells. Both *rosea* and the white variety *alba* are beautiful. Their worst enemy are slugs and it is a good plan to surround the plants with collars of perforated zinc to protect them from destruction by these pests. 12, 13, 60, 82, 84.

LARKSPUR. Annual delphiniums, invaluable hardy plants, best sown in boxes and planted out. Many colours are offered by seedsmen in both stock-flowered and hyacinth-flowered varieties. 29, 39, 58.

LATHYRUS LATIFOLIUS. Everlasting pea. White Pearl is a fine variety. 40.

LAVENDER (*Lavandula*). A dwarf shrub thriving particularly in chalky soil. As well as the lilac-coloured variety there are a white and also one or two dwarf varieties. 27, 50.

LILAC (*Syringa*). Lilacs like generous treatment, and it is well to remove the faded flower trusses to prevent seed formation, which tends to exhaust the plant. The following are good varieties: Marie Legraye, single white. Madame Lemoine and Miss Ellen Willmott, double white. Souvenir de Louis Späth, single deep purple. Michael Buchner, double pale lilac. 13, 14, 26, 32, 42, 92, 103.

LILIUM.

L. auratum. The golden-rayed lily of Japan. 66.

L. candidum or Madonna lily. The old-fashioned white garden lily blooming in June. 36, 37.

L. giganteum. A lily for woodland growing up to 10 and 12 ft. with many flowers on a stem. The finest of all lilies. 37.

L. Krameri or *japonicum*. Difficult to establish out of doors, is lovely as a cool greenhouse plant. 56, 63, 84.

L. longiflorum. The well-known white trumpet lily. 26, 27, 31, 81, 105.

L. Martagon album. The white Turk's-cap lily. Growing 4 ft. high when freely established and bearing many heads of waxy-white reflexed flowers. 37.

L. Martagon dalmaticum. A fine garden lily. Deep wine-purple, growing 6 ft. high when well established. 56, 57.

L. monadelphum. A beautiful yellow garden lily with reflexed flowers which hang from the stems.

L. monadelphum szovitzianium. A beautiful form with pale-yellow flowers spotted with deep purple. 63.

LILIUM—*continued*
L. *nepalense*. A rare greenish-white lily, suitable for a bed in a cool greenhouse. 48.
L. *regale*. 31.
L. *speciosum rubrum*. A variety of L. *speciosum*, rose-pink in colour. 27.
L. *tenuifolium*. 29.
L. *testaceum*. The Nankeen lily, a beautiful garden variety. The growth something like L. *candidum*, and in colour a delicate apricot yellow. 63.
L. *umbellatum*. 69.
L. *Willmottiae*. 69.
LILY OF THE VALLEY or *Convallaria*. 12, 13.
LIME TREE. 48.
LOBELIA CARDINALIS. 58.
LOVE-LIES-BLEEDING (*Amaranthus caudatus*). A hardy annual. Seed is best sown in boxes and the seedlings planted out. Both red and white varieties are worth growing for cut flowers. 15, 27, 47, 57.
LUPIN. 27, 29, 45, 65.
LYCHNIS. Rose Campion. Good scarlet hardy perennials. 58.
LYTHRUM. Loosestrife. A hardy perennial. L. *virgatum* is purple in colour, a good border variety. 53.
MACLURA. A deciduous tree seldom seen in this country. Bearing inedible green fruits of great decorative value. 49.
MAGNOLIA. Magnificent flowering shrubs and trees, both hardy and half-hardy. 32.
M. *conspicua*. The Yulan tree, white, scented, flowers in spring, March to May. The flowers come before the leaves, creating an almost dramatic effect. 41, 82.
M. *Fraseri*. Flowers in May and June, yellowish-white, about 8 in. across. The seed-head is rose-coloured. 67.
M. *grandiflora*. The beautiful shiny-leaved evergreen, usually seen growing on houses. Large, creamy-white scented flowers in late summer and autumn. The Exmouth variety is said to be hardier and to flower younger. 41, 49.
M. *parviflora*. 41.
M. *soulangeana nigra*. Flowers white inside and purple outside, in April. 16.
M. *stellata*. 41.
M. *Watsoni*. Scented white flowers tinged rose on outside of petals, crimson petals. June and July. 41.
MAIDENHAIR FERN (*Adiantum cuneatum*). Greenhouse ferns. 50.
MALLOW. 13, 39.
MARIGOLD, AFRICAN. Annuals. 15, 29.
MARROW. 14, 49.
MECONOPSIS BAILEYI, the blue poppy from Tibet. A perennial, more safely treated as a biennial as it often dies off after flowering. 29, 74, 75.
MEDLARS. 45.
MEGASEA. Belonging to the saxifrage family. Large-leaved, spring-flowering plants. Flowers pale and deep bluish-pink, borne on stout stems, pretty and early. 58.
MISTLETOE. 90.
MONARDA DIDYMA. Sweet Bergamot. Hardy perennial. Scarlet flowers and deliciously scented leaves. 58.
MOSS. 106.
MOUNTAIN ASH. 34.
MUSCARI. Small bulbous plants including grape and feathered hyacinths. 22, 76, 77.
MYRTLE. Evergreen aromatic shrubs with white flowers. They need some shelter. 33, 86.
NARCISSUS. 12.
NASTURTIUM. 17, 22, 26, 27, 68.
NERINE. 84.
NETTLE, STINGING. 46.
NIGELLA. Love-in-a-mist. 45.
N. *damascena*. Blue. 39.
N. *damascena alba*. White. 13, 39.
N. *damascena Miss Jekyll*. A very good blue. 74.
Hispanica has decorative seed-pods. 39.
ONION FLOWERS. 45, 51.
ORANGE BLOSSOM. 81.
ORNITHOGALUM. 34, 38.
PAMPAS GRASS. *Grandiflorum* is a fine white variety, and *roseum* has shell-pink plumes. 59.
PANCRATIUM. Bulbous greenhouse plants with beautiful white flowers. 43.

APPENDIX

PANSY. 28.
PASSION FLOWER (*Passiflora*). Almost hardy climbers. *Caerulea*, blue and white. Constance Elliott, white. 14, 42, 74.
PASSION FRUIT. 17.
PEAS. 14.
PELARGONIUM. 43, 79.
PENTSTEMON. 40, 53, 78.
PEONY. 14, 17, 27, 31, 40, 58, 71, 92.
  Peony. Countess Cadogan. 42.
PERNETTYA. Low-growing evergreen shrubs, valuable for red, pink, and white berries. 33.
PERSIMMON. 64.
PETUNIA. 27, 78.
PHILADELPHUS. 13, 31, 32, 42.
PHLOX. Herbaceous phloxes, late summer- and autumn-flowering. 13, 15, 27, 53. *Annual phloxes* (half-hardy). Should be sown in boxes in gentle heat. Good distinct colours may be had. 68, 74, 78.
  Phlox species. There are many good species in pinks, mauves, and whites. Especially suitable for rock work.
  P. Laphami is a good variety with lavender-blue flowers suitable for cutting. 22, 75.
PHYTOLACCA DECANDRA. Hardy herbaceous perennial, valuable for its purple berries in long terminal clusters. 73, 74.
PINKS. 13, 20, 28.
  Pinks. Rock. 28.
PLUMBAGO CAPENSIS. Greenhouse shrub bearing phlox-shaped flowers of an unusual shade of pale blue in summer and autumn. There is also a white variety. 22, 74.
POINSETTIA. Warm greenhouse plant. The brilliant scarlet leaf-bracts look like flowers. Much used at Christmas time. There are pale-pink and white varieties not often seen. 103.
POLYANTHUS. 21, 74, 78.
POPPIES. Perennial. 40, 57, 70.
  Poppies. Annual. 13, 27, 54, 70, 73.
  Poppies. White Swan and purple. 39.
POPPY HEADS. 14, 15.
PRIMROSE. Blue. 21, 76.

PRIMULAS. 70.
  P. sikkimensis. Two feet, yellow, summer-flowering primula. 71.
PRIVET. Berries. 34.
PRUNUS. Ornamental trees. Valuable for flowers and fruit. 26.
PYRUS. Ornamental trees valuable for blossom and fruit. 26.
  P. japonica. 14.
QUINCE. 28, 45.
RHEUM (Rhubarb). Large decorative subjects, *Alexandrae, tanghuticum*. 45, 66.
RHODODENDRON. 27, 31, 59, 92.
RIBES. White. 42.
RICHARDIA (*Africana*). The white arum lily. *Elliottiana*. Golden yellow with spotted foliage. 17, 27, 29, 83.
RICINUS. Half-hardy annual. Valuable for ornamental foliage. 57.
ROSEMARY. 50.
ROSES. 28, 29, 54, 55, 60, 83, 103.
  Butterfly. 27.
  Cabbage. 20, 27.
  Frau Karl Druschki. 14, 27, 31.
  Gloire de Dijon. 20, 68.
  La France. 60.
  Maréchal Niel. Pale-yellow greenhouse rose. 83.
  Moss. 60.
  Niphetos. The Bridal Rose, pure and delicate white, needs a sheltered position or may be grown in greenhouse. 43, 83.
  White. 12, 13, 46, 73.
  Rosa Hugonis. 71.
RUBUS BIFLORUS. The whitewashed bramble. 43.
SALPIGLOSSIS. 70.
SALVIA. 15.
  S. patens. The blue species with intense blue flowers in summer and autumn, not quite hardy and may be treated as dahlias.
  S. virgata nemorosa. Hardy herbaceous species bearing purple flowers. 78.
SANTOLINA INCANA (Lavender Cotton). A pretty silvery-white foliage shrub. 50.
SAXIFRAGE. 12.
SCABIOUS. 15, 27, 85.
SCILLA. 76.

SEAKALE. 40, 51.
SEED-HEADS. 45, 46, 49, 50, 64, 65.
SIDALCEA. 58.
SINO-FRANCHETTIA CHINENSIS. Purple-berried climber. 74.
SNAPDRAGON.
SNOWBERRY (*Symphoricarpus laevigatus*). 14.
SOLOMON'S SEAL. 17.
SORREL. 45.
SPIREA. 42, 68.
 S. ariaefolia. 65.
STATICE. 65.
STEPHANOTIS. Greenhouse climber bearing scented waxen flowers. 12, 13, 32, 82.
STERNBERGIA LUTEA. A hardy bulb bearing yellow crocus-like flowers in autumn. Likes sharp drainage and warm border. 28, 63.
STOCK. 26, 58, 68, 70.
STRAWBERRIES (Wild). 28.
STREPTOSOLON. Yellow greenhouse climber. 29, 71.
SWEET PEA. 85.
SWEET ROCKET (*Hesperis matronalis*). Single varieties purple and white, best treated as biennials, sweet-scented in the evening. Double white, an old-fashioned favourite not as easy to grow as single varieties. Propagation by division of crowns. Likes moisture below roots. 40.
SWEET SULTAN. 39, 70.
SWEET WILLIAM. 20, 28.
SYMPHORICARPUS (Snowberry). 14, 27, 33, 34, 51.
SYRINGA. See Philadelphus.
TEAZLE. 65.
THALICTRUM DIPTEROCARPUM. Hardy herbaceous perennial with purple flowers 3 to 4 feet high. 78.
THISTLE. 16, 26, 29.
 Globe. 27.
 Palestine, *Onopordon Salterii.* 50.
THYME. 21.
TOADSTOOLS. 23, 68.

TOMATOES. Ornamental varieties. Plum, cherry, and currant in both red and yellow. 14, 15, 23, 26, 28, 49, 61.
TRAVELLER'S JOY. *Clematis vitalba.* 46.
TRITOMA. 45.
TRITONIA. 29, 83.
TROLLIUS. 29.
TUBEROSE. 13, 15, 38, 51.
TULIPS. 12, 26, 27, 29, 39, 68, 77.
 Carrara. 39.
 Lord Carnarvon. 55.
 Moonlight. 69.
 Parrot. 26, 69.
 Safrano. 67.
 Sirene. 55, 84.
 T. Clusiana. 55, 56.
 T. Griegii. 55, 56.
 T. retroflexa. 29.
 T. viridiflora. 17, 47.
TYPHA ANGUSTIFOLIA. A small form of bulrush liking marshy ground. Good for winter decoration. 68.
VERBENA. Half-hardy perennial. The hybrids have brilliantly coloured flowers in many shades; they bloom profusely in summer and autumn. 15, 21, 54, 70, 78.
 Verbena. Lemon-scented. 50.
VERONICA. 22, 29, 74.
VIBURNUM. 48.
 Viburnum Carlesii. Beautiful deciduous shrub bearing fragrant white flowers in May. 41.
VINES. 73, 105.
VIOLA. 13.
VIOLET. 21, 28.
WATER LILY or *Nymphaea.* Water-lily blue. A beautiful lily for the greenhouse tank or will bloom out of doors in summer if taken into the greenhouse for winter months. 14, 22, 74.
WILLOW-HERB. *Epilobium.* 53, 54.
WISTARIA. *Glycine.* Hardy deciduous climber. *Sinensis,* mauve flowers. *Alba,* white flowers, very sweet-scented. 42.
YARROW. 65.
YUCCA. 67.
ZINNIA. 15, 27, 51, 53, 68, 70.

ILLUSTRATIONS
FROM PHOTOGRAPHS BY PAUL LAIB

White Table
Decoration wit
White China

Refer to pages 13, 21, and

Alabaster Bowl
with Red Roses

refer to pages 13, 54, 95, and 97

123

Green Table
Decoration with
Fruit and Flower

Shell of
Nasturtium

124

Refer to pages 14, 17, 22, 49, 75, and

WALL VASE WITH
MIXED BUNCH

Refer to pages 27, 91, and 98

125

ALABASTER ON
BLACK STAND WITH
MIXED BUNCH

Refer to pages 27, 78, and 97

ALABASTER WITH GRAPES
AND WHITE ROSES

'Chromatic'
painting by Gluck

Black Bowl with
Rhododendron
Flower Heads

Low Alabaster Vase
with Mixed Bunch

Refer to pages 31, 60, 97, and 10

Celadon Bowl with
Philadelphus (Syringa) Blossom

Refer to page 31

BLACK MARBLE BOWL
WITH
DOUBLE SYRINGA

Refer to pages 32 and 97

BASKET OF GOURDS

SEAKALE IN FLOWER

Refer to pages 40 and

Tall Glass Vase
with Single White
Rose, Laburnum
Seeds, etc.

Refer to page 46

WARWICK VASE
WITH GREEN
LOVE-LIES-BLEEDING

Dracunculus
  in Glass Vase

Griffin with
Dried Mixtur

Refer to pages 65 and 9

COPPER JUG WITH HUMEA AND DAY-LILIES

Refer to page 66

Pottery Vase with
Rhubarb and
Spurge

STRIPPED ELDERBERRY

Corky Stem in
Glass Cornucopi

Dead Group in
Black Marble Vase

refer to page 65

143

Stick of Longi-
florum Lilies

Hand Spray of
   Arum Lilies

refer to page 82

145

Hand Spray of
White Camellia

Refer to page 8

ctorian Bouquet
of Camellias

r to page 82

Artificial

Christmas Tr

Refer to pages 90 and

FORMAL ARUMS IN
MARBLE VASE

Refer to pages 96 and 101

149

GROUP OF YELLOW
FLOWERS AND FRU[IT]
IN LEAD VASE

Grapes in
Alabaster Vase
with Black Base

Refer to pages 95 and 97

Pink Shell with
Tulips